Hel
D1644872

THE SPIRIT OF TOLERANCE

THE SPIRIT OF TOLERANCE

edited and arranged
by

KATHARINE MOORE

with a foreword by
VICTOR GOLLANCZ

VICTOR GOLLANCZ LTD

LONDON · MDCCCCLXIV

MADE AND PRINTED IN GREAT BRITAIN BY
THE GARDEN CITY PRESS LIMITED
LETCHWORTH, HERTFORDSHIRE

To

H. M., J. K. K.

AND

C. K. Y. M.

IN LOVE AND GRATITUDE

CONTENTS

P. 231 on – Interestings notes on auth

FOREWORD

I cannot imagine why I undertook to write this foreword: for one should practise what one preaches, and while I am among the most tolerant of men when the largest matters are at issue (and in the abstract), I am at the other extreme when it comes to the smaller details of concrete daily living. While strongly disapproving, for instance, of cannibalism, I am tolerant of it—I can enter into the cannibal's point of view: but I find it extremely difficult to keep my temper with a man who enjoys turtle soup, even if I know that he is totally ignorant of the barbarity involved. Similarly, I have always been tolerant of murderers, for all my horrified sympathy with their victims: but I have to struggle long and hard before I can bring myself to pass the time of day with a fox-hunter.

The reason for this paradox is clear. I passionately *believe* in tolerance: when the need for it hits me in the depths I immediately and instinctively respond: but on lesser occasions my egoism conquers my agape—what *Gollancz* feels about it affects him more than what ought to be his fellow-feeling with all humanity. Which is another way of saying that perfect tolerance can be achieved only by a love far greater than I have been able to manage.

So much by way of apologia.

§ 2

The spirit of tolerance is the spirit of respect for personality, the social value of values.

The words "respect" and "personality" in the phrase "respect for personality" require definition. Respect does not mean (as it means when used with a narrower significance) admiring, or fearing, or looking up to, or dutifully obeying, or regarding as good, or recognizing as superior in character or intellect or station; nor does it mean some or all of these attitudes, or of similar attitudes, combined in various proportions. And "personality" does not mean "certain selected personalities".

Negatively, respect for personality can be understood by reflecting on a statement that uses the word "respect" in one of the narrower senses. Consider, for instance, the phrase "I respect my father". If anyone who said that were asked "Why?" he would probably answer "Because he's my father". Further pressed, he might insist that the reason was sufficient, or might be prepared to amend his reply to "Because he's a good father". Similarly, a man might say "I respect the Queen: because she is the Queen: because she has carried out with courage and devotion the duties of a constitutional monarch". Or, rather differently, "I respect Mr. Churchill, not because he was Prime Minister nor yet because I agreed with his politics, but because during the most critical years of our history, and with a burden of responsibility such as no other Englishman has ever borne, he had the faith of a child and the heart of a lion".

Now the very fact that in these sentences my father, the Queen, and Mr. Churchill are *selected* as objects of respect shows that the word "respect" is being used in a sense other and narrower than that which we intend when we speak of "respect for personality": and this at once becomes apparent when such reasons as "because he's my father" or "because he's a good father" are adduced in explanation. The very reason for which we respect them in the broader sense would itself preclude us from *particularizing* them for respect in that sense. I personally do in fact respect, in the narrower sense also, all three of them (retrospectively, in my father's case); but if I were asked "Why do you respect your father, and the Queen, and Mr. Churchill?", and if I understood that respect in the broader sense were intended, my reply in all three cases would be the same, namely, "because they are persons".

When we say that we respect personality, we mean that we recognize in every human being, and to a certain extent (or even completely, perhaps) in every living thing, something special, particular, concrete, individual, unique: something, as the Greeks would have said, αὐτὸ καθ' αὔτο: something—and this is perhaps the nearest that can be got to expressing what from its very nature must elude definition—something in its own right. There is in every human being, we say, something as much in *his* own right as my self-consciousness tells me I am in *mine*.

As much as I am in mine, but no more; for I also am a personality that I must respect. Fénelon, anticipating Freud (as so often theology, from its different approach, anticipated modern psychology) said somewhere that we should be in charity with ourselves as well as with our neighbours. There is indeed nothing self-abasing in respect for personality. In spite of *accidental* differences, and very wide ones, in spiritual development—the difference, for instance, between St. Francis at one end of the scale and Herr Hitler at the other; in spite, too, of greatly varying levels of capacity and intellect: respect for personality recognizes the *essential* spiritual equality of all human beings, including ourselves, and perhaps of every living thing.

If I have made myself clear, it must at once be apparent that the real test of respect for personality is our attitude towards people we "don't like", towards those whom, in the narrower sense, we "don't respect", and to all whom we think of as enemies or criminals or sinners. To be concrete, and to avoid contemporary examples, the test was our attitude, during the war, to Germans and Italians and Japanese; a little later, to William Joyce; a little later still, to Goering and Ribbentrop and Streicher and the rest. To talk of Huns and Wops: to rejoice when Joyce was sentenced to a shameful end: to think with pleasurable triumph of those wretched men in the dock at Nuremberg—all this was to blaspheme against respect for personality.

I remember reading as a boy something written by Oscar Wilde—I think it is in *De Profundis*—which made a profound impression on me. Wilde had been tried and sentenced; and as he left the dock for prison, when everywhere around him was an atmosphere of hostility and contempt, a bearded stranger, whom he was never to see again (I believe it was Bernard Shaw), raised his hat in salutation. He did this, I like to think, not because he sympathized with Wilde's practices, nor because he disapproved of the sentence, but as a simple act of respect to a fellow human being in torment.

Only one person on earth, so far as the records go, has shown a respect for personality utter and without reservation. Christ consorted with harlots and sinners neither in condescension nor without recognition of their sins: he thought of them quite naturally, quite as a matter of course one might say, as fellow human beings, and therefore, to him as a man, essentially and beyond their sins his equals. "Why callest thou me good?" he asked: "there is none good but one, that is, God." And he preached respect for personality in words of a beauty and conviction that never have been and never can be surpassed. There is some great music—Beethoven's Fifth Symphony, for instance—which over-familiarity has spoiled: only when a Klemperer conducts it, or when there is a magic fitting of the music to our need, does it mean for us what it meant when we were young and freshly receptive to its message. So only when they are spoken by a voice of great spiritual power, or when at some climax of disgrace, such as Belsen or Hiroshima or Birmingham Alabama, we fly to what may save us from terror and despair—only at moments such as these do we experience once again the full revelation of verses which teach respect for personality in its ultimate form—the verses that begin with the words "But I say unto you, love your enemies".

But *why*, it may be asked, should we respect personality—not this or that personality, but personality as such? What is the sanction? There are many answers: one, and an obvious one, would be given by pantheism, and others by various systems of eastern wisdom and western philosophy. But there are two answers, I think, that come naturally to people trained in the European tradition; and they are not, as will be seen, mutually exclusive. They may be loosely called the religious and the non-religious.

In western religious thought, respect for personality is demanded by three interrelated religious doctrines: that God created all men in His own image, that God is the Father of all men, and that all men are therefore brothers. Both before and after the birth of Christianity, Judaism—prophetic, talmudic and cabbalistic—insisted on this Fatherhood of God and brotherhood of men. "Are ye not" cries the prophet Amos—"Are ye not as children of the Ethiopians unto me, O children of Israel? saith the Lord. Have not I brought up Israel out of the land of Egypt? and the Philistines from Caphtor, and the

Syrians from Kir?" Which is as if a Jewish survivor from Auschwitz were to ask "Is not my God also the God of the Nazis?" There is a legend in the Talmud that is remarkable not so much for what it says as for the light it throws on the religious consciousness of men who, regarding Egypt as the national enemy, could nevertheless invent it. The story runs like this: that when the Egyptians were drowning in the Red Sea, and Miriam was singing her song of triumph and thanksgiving, the angels in heaven began to take up the refrain; but God stopped them, saying "What? My children are drowning, and ye would rejoice?" To this day orthodox Jews preserve the memory of that legend. It is customary on all joyful occasions to sing the Hallel, or song of praise. But during Passover, which commemorates the deliverance from Egypt, it is sung in full only on the first three days; on the four remaining days it is sung in a shortened form, because some thirty-three centuries ago the Egyptians, who were also God's children, were destroyed. In the same spirit, but even more directly, the Cabbala insists that every man, however sinful, is in some degree divine. With that mixture of nonsense and profound wisdom which is characteristic of it, it relates that God has divided Himself and placed a particle of Himself in the soul of every human being: and that there it will remain, pure and undefiled no matter how wicked the individual may be, until men, reuniting with one another in perfect brotherhood, recreate at last the Unity of God.

But it was Christ who was to experience the universality of God's Fatherhood with a directness and immediacy never approached before or since. Or if that is too bold a claim, for no one can know what is in other men's hearts, it is at least true to say that he alone has had the power to communicate some measure of this experience to countless others. "Are not two sparrows," he asked, "sold for a farthing? and one of them shall not fall on the ground without your Father." I have already suggested that in the injunction to love our enemies respect for personality finds its ultimate expression. And we are immediately told *why* we should love our enemies: "That ye may be the children of your Father which is in heaven: for he maketh his sun to rise on the evil and on the good, and sendeth rain on the just and on the unjust." These few words, so rebuking to the self-righteous, are the greatest of all Christ's gifts—the greatest of all the gifts, I would dare to say, of Hebrew prophecy—to the religion of the western world.

The non-religious man of our tradition, if asked why we should respect personality, would give a different answer, though many may think that it is in the last analysis the same. I recognize (he would say), with a sense of necessity or inevitability independent of logical processes, my own uniqueness, my own "being in my own right". I recognize that there is in me an inner citadel that must be for ever inviolate. And because I recognize this I understand, by imaginative sympathy, that what is true of me is true of others: that every human being is unique, and has a citadel which is sacred: and that I must imperatively respect in others what I know, from the very nature of my being, must be respected in me.

§ 3

The antithesis of respect, and the grossly final expression of disrespect, for personality is violence, the disease of our age. In calling it that I am not thinking only of the "balance of terror" in international relations, or of the current contempt for pacifism, or of teenage hooliganism: I am thinking also of cruelty on the cinema and television screen and in the theatre, and of what amounts to the brutally mechanical in a great deal of contemporary art. And I am thinking, above all, of the sort of literature, put out by reputable publishers and praised by reputable critics, for which almost alone (and as a publisher myself I know what I am talking about) a great sale can nowadays be safely guaranteed.

The question is not one of pornography, the better sort of which, in a poor second-hand sort of way, is to some degree life-enhancing: like the aroma that might faintly come through to a tramp at the half-open door of an expensive restaurant. I am told, for instance, that *Fanny Hill* can give a mild kind of pleasure to anyone except a puritan. The bogus-highbrow kind of filth I have in mind, on the other hand (and its publication has proliferated horribly), is life-denying: spiritually as well as physically disgusting and tasteless to an almost incredible degree, it offends against value of any kind (including intellectual value) every bit as much as against public decency. And the point is this: seeing everything in terms of brutal mechanism, it offends, most of all, against respect for personality, which is essentially spiritual. A few months ago a novel was specially recommended by its publisher in a huge newspaper advertisement for its "violence and sex": that is a startling indication of how far things have gone.

The contemporary climate of violence must endanger everything of value on this earth, and there is only one way to check it: namely, to foster the spiritual, to respect human—human-divine—personality.

V. G.

PREFACE

In this anthology I have tried to show what is the nature of true tolerance, and have arranged the chosen passages in a particular order to illustrate this. The headings and introductions to each section indicate the growth towards the final merging of tolerance into love.

Sir Richard Livingstone has said that "tolerance has always been needed for the happiness and well-being of the human race. Today it is needed for survival". There is no need, therefore, to apologize for an anthology in praise of Tolerance, but all anthologies are the result of a personal choice, and some who may read this one will perhaps be incensed at certain omissions or inclusions.

A member of the State legislature of Alabama is reported as having said, "There are two things that I cannot stand; one is intolerance and the other is niggers". Perhaps most of us feel that all intolerance is wrong except that of our own particular aversions. If then I have offended by my personal choice I can only ask for tolerance towards myself.

The focus of intolerance varies from age to age. Today, racial bitterness has largely replaced religious intolerance, but the spirit of tolerance remains the same and in that sense nothing here is out of date. The passages in each section are naturally only a representative selection, and especially is this the case in those illustrating charity towards the weak and exploited, which are drawn from a very wide field. I was tempted to include animals here, but this would have widened it still further.

Finally I would say with William Chillingworth, "And besides in the framing of this building tho I were the only architect, yet I wanted not the assistance of diligent hands to bring me in choice materials towards it, nor of careful and watchful eyes to correct the errors of my work".

I wish to thank those diligent hands, whether I have made use of what they brought or not, and more especially am I grateful to my husband for "his careful and watchful eyes".

Katharine Moore

FIRST PART

THE OPEN MIND

The tolerant man is the man of vision. His mind is open to the constant interplay of differing ideas and to the enrichment that comes from variety of experience. Most important, he is forced to discriminate, to contrast, to choose, and, from all this ferment, new ideas are born.

It is only through tolerance of varying and even opposing thought that growth is possible. Freedom of thought is necessary for any step forward. So the man of tolerance has often proved a true prophet. He has, in his day, patiently defended the despised, the outrageous, the persecuted; many times with little or no success. Yet, in time, what was held to be intolerable has become not only widely accepted but essential.

Which has proved to be right over race relations, child labour, Ireland, Catholic Emancipation, women's place in society, the recognition of genius—John Woolman or Carlyle, Shaftesbury or his opponents, Fox or George III, Erasmus or Luther, the tiny number who applauded Keats or the *Quarterly*? In a word, the tolerant or the intolerant?

I

Variety of Experience and Thought

Tis by succession of delight
That Love supports his reign.

Christopher Smart

Truth exists only in boundless communication.

Karl Jaspers

"They must often change," says Confucius, "who would be constant in happiness or wisdom."

Oliver Goldsmith

Let us not look back in anger nor forward in fear but around in awareness.

James Thurber

In defence of Images

For God Himself, the father and creator of all things, is more ancient than the sun and the heavens, greater than Time and eternity and all the flow of life, is a legislator without law, unutterable by any voice, invisible to any eye. But we, being unable to comprehend His essence, use words and names to help us, and animals, figures of gold and ivory and silver, plants and rivers, mountain summits and streams, longing to know Him, but in our weakness calling Him by all that appears to us to be beautiful. And in doing thus we act like lovers. To these the actual vision of the beloved is the most beautiful sight possible but for their sake they will delight in a lyre, in a dart, a chair, or the race course in which they ran or anything that calls to mind the beloved. Why should I pass any further judgment about Images? Let them know what is divine, that is all. But if the art of Phidias excites the Greeks to the recollection of God, the worship of animals, the Egyptians, and others are inspired by a river or by a fire—I do not condemn nor am angered by their differences; let them only know, let them only love, let them remember.

Maximus of Tyre: *Dissertations*

Recently I was shown two little idols given to a missionary by a young convert (from a famous family)—his own idols: two delightful little idols the size of my hand, carved in hard wood. One represented a jolly, rather pot-bellied Buddha stepping out in a light-hearted dance. The other was a female Buddha, praying, a little marvel of human and heavenly beauty. In the first there was nothing spiritually interesting . . . but the second held the real fragrance of prayer. . . . There is a vast quantity of goodness and beauty outside the Church, which will come to fruition, no doubt, only in Christ; meanwhile they are still there, and we must give them our sympathy if we are to be fully Christian ourselves. . . . The more I knock about, the more aware I become of the richness and variety of the lives and temperaments that we try to force into the same mould.

Pierre Teilhard de Chardin: *Letters from a Traveller*

No fence round God

The old pagans of my time had seen the emissaries of the new faith working ruthlessly against their loved ancestors in the earlier days of missionary work, and for that reason most of them resisted to the end every effort to Christianize them. But they distinguished with extraordinary sensitiveness between the new God and His human prophets. . . . So Katutu, a pagan of about eighty, put it to me at Tarawa. "And besides, God and Jesus do not belong only to the Protestants and Roman Catholics," he said to me. "They belong to pagans also. They are not surrounded by a fence up there in Heaven, and we do not have to run into a mission fence to find them here on earth. They are everywhere, like Anriaria and Tabuariki and Tituaabine. We can take them for our own friends if we want them." And some of them did precisely that, by the simple expedient of using the names of God and Jesus as names of power in their magic of kindness.

Arthur Grimble: *A Pattern of Islands*

Ought it to be assumed that in all men the mixture of religion with other elements should be identical? Ought it, indeed, to be assumed that the lives of all men should show identical religious elements? In other words, is the existence of so many religious types and sects and creeds regrettable?

To these questions I answer "No" emphatically. And my reason is that I do not see how it is possible that creatures in such different positions and with such different powers as human individuals are should have exactly the same functions and the same duties. No two of us have identical difficulties, nor should we be expected to work out identical solutions. Each, from his peculiar angle of observation, takes in a certain sphere of fact and trouble, which each must deal with in a unique manner. . . . The divine can mean no single quality, it must mean a group of qualities, by being champions of which in alternation, different men may all find worthy missions. Each attitude being a syllable in human nature's total message, it takes the whole of us to spell the meaning out completely. So a "god of battles" must be allowed to be the god for one kind of person, a god of peace and heaven and home the god for another. We must frankly recognize the fact that we live in partial systems, and that parts are not interchangeable in the spiritual life. If we are peevish and jealous, destruction of the self must be an element of our religion; why need it be one if we are good and sympathetic from the outset? If we are sick souls, we require a religion of deliverance; but why think so much of deliverance, if we are healthy-minded? Unquestionably, some men have the completer experience and the higher vocation, here just as in the social world; but for each man to stay in his own experience, whate'er it be, and for others to tolerate him there, is surely best.

William James: *The Varieties of Religious Experience*

All the surface part of religion, that is all the spectacular part and the emotional part, are largely matters of geography and of race, and also I would say of era too. But behind and beneath all these there is a knowledge of God that must be and that is more or less the same everywhere. I like Jukes's illustration taken from the description of the Holy City in Revelation. The city lieth "four-square" and has gates on every side. Consequently people who enter it come from all the four corners of the earth and travel in four opposite directions. The man who enters one gate must travel south while the man who enters the opposite gate must travel north. But all enter the city and meet there. And just so in finding God. We may travel on exactly opposite pathways according to our race, or country, or era, but we all meet in God at last. I fully agree with thee about the ticklishness of our emotions, and therefore that gate of entrance would never be the one for me, although I believe many do enter there.

Mrs. Pearsall Smith: *Letters*

O never rudely will I blame his faith
In the might of stars and angels! 'Tis not merely
The human being's pride that peoples space
With life and mystical predominance;
Since likewise for the stricken heart of Love
This visible nature, and this common world,
Is all too narrow: yea, a deeper import
Lurks in the legend told my infant years
Than lies upon that truth, we live to learn.
For fable is Love's world, his home, his birthplace:
Delightedly dwells he 'mong fays, and talismans,
And spirits; and delightedly believes
Divinities, being himself divine.
The intelligible forms of ancient poets,
The fair humanities of old religion,
The power, the beauty and the majesty,
That had their haunts in dale, or piny mountain,
Or forest by slow stream, or pebbly spring,
Or chasms and wat'ry depths; all these have vanished.
They live no longer in the faith of reason!
But still the heart doth need a language, still
Doth the old instinct bring back the old names.
And to yon starry world they now are gone,
Spirits or gods, that used to share this earth
With man as with their friend, . . .

S. T. Coleridge: *The Piccolomini*

In such a mighty contest, sedition and discord, you will see one according law and assertion in all the earth, that there is one God, the King and father of all things, and many gods, sons of God, ruling together with him. This the Greek says, and the barbarian says, the inhabitant of the continent, and he who dwells near the sea, the wise and the unwise. And if you proceed as far as to the uttermost shores of the ocean, there, also, there are gods, rising very near to some, and setting very near to others. Do you think Plato opposes, or prescribes laws contrary to these, and that he does not accord with this most beautiful assertion, and most true affection of the human mind? What is this? The eye says it is the sun. What is that? The ear says it is thunder. What are these things thus flourishing and beautiful? The soul says, that all these are the works of divinity; it desires the creator and predicts his art.

. . . But if you are blind to the vision of the Creator of all things, it may suffice you at present to survey his works, and adore his offspring, which are many and all various; and not only those which the Boeotian poet enumerates. For there are not only thirty thousand gods, the sons and friends of God, but the multitude of divine essences is innumerable.

Maximus of Tyre: *Dissertations*

Tolerance of differing Values

During my salad days as a District Officer, my closest friend Mantake-Macke . . . read me a sound lesson in what you might call the doctrine of compensating values.

. . . It appeared that [a certain] Tabanea was a professional wizard famed throughout the Gilbert Islands for "the magic of kindness". He dealt exclusively in spells, amulets and potions that brought good luck and protection against enemy sorcerers.

. . . "and so," said Mantake, "Tabanea sends a message before him when he is about to pass through a village: and the people bring gifts of money . . . then Tabanea renews his bonota [protective spell] over their village and everyone is happy."

"But, Mantake," I exclaimed, "this thing must be stopped at

once." He looked at me blankly: "How?" he said, "I don't understand."

"The thing must be stopped," I repeated.

"Why?"

"Because the man's levying a kind of tax on the villagers."

"He levies no tax," Mantake replied firmly. "The people want his help, and pay for it in advance. What he does makes them happy."

"But do you believe that they are any the safer for his spells?"

"What I believe or you believe is of no account," was his notable reply. "They believe. Only that matters. They believe and so they are happy, and because they are happy they are safe."

"But," I protested, "most of the villagers are baptised Protestants or Roman Catholics. Why should so great a majority be forced to pay Tabanea a tribute just because a few pagans still fear the wawi?"

He smiled: "The Christians want Tabanea's protection as much as the pagans. Nobody is obliged to pay anything: nor is it known who pays or who refuses."

"[But] Tabanea is, in the end of things, levying a toll on the villagers."

"And the missionaries?" Mantake questioned, and paused.

"Well? What about them?"

"Only this. The missionaries bring us their prayers and their schools, and they ask for gifts in return. We think that is just; we are happy to have them among us; so we give them much money. And then? Does the government step in to prevent us? Does the government measure the gifts we give? Does the government accuse the missionaries of levying a tax upon us? . . . And so," he continued, "if you punish those who are willing to sell tabunea [spells] for good luck . . . where will they go to find magic for good eating and good sleeping . . . for finding out their lucky days and their unlucky days, for making their wives fruitful and their children strong, for all the comforts between dawn and dawn that the magic of kindness brings them?"

His words meant in effect that the magic of kindness filled the life of his people, Christians and pagans alike, with a mass of daily interests for the sudden loss of which nothing that the white man gave or sold could properly compensate them. He was specific on the point of compensating values: "If the government or missionaries could give them something to keep their hearts alive night and day even as the magic of kindness does, perhaps they could be happy without Tabanea and his like," he said. "But if you cannot give them an equal thing in return, you will kill their hearts by robbing them of their loved wizards."

Of course he was right: His wisdom saved me from an error I should never have ceased to rue. I did nothing whatever about Tabanea except to seek his acquaintance. He was a fine, kindly old gentleman, whose contribution to the easier passage of his people through the psychological darkness between paganism and Christianity I learned to appreciate deeply.

Arthur Grimble: *A Pattern of Islands*

A man who is a really good man may live well in any kind of life. But it may be that you deem it a blessed thing to die at a good age in the midst of your brotherhood. This is a notion which deceives and deludes not you alone, but almost everybody. We think that Christ and religion consists in certain places and garments and modes of life, and ceremonial observances. It is all up, we think, with a man who changes his white habit for a black one, or who substitutes a hat for a hood, and who frequently changes his residence. . . . How much more in accordant to the teaching of Christ would it be to look upon all Christendom as one home; as it were one monastery; to regard all men as canons and brothers . . . not to care where you live, if only you live well!

Erasmus: *Letter to Servetus*

A traveller's indifference to the way by which he may reach his goal

For my desire is to go the right way to eternal happiness. But whether it be by following a living guide, or by seeking my direction in a Book, or by hearkening to the secret whisper of some private Spirit, to me is indifferent. And he that is otherwise affected, and hath not a traveller's indifference, which Epictetus requires in all that would find the truth, but much desires in respect of his ease or pleasure or profit or advancement, or satisfaction of friends, or any humane consideration, that one way should be true rather than another; it is odds but he will take his desire that it should be so for an assurance that it is so. But I for my part, unless I deceive myself was and am still so affected as I have made profession, not willing I confess to take anything upon trust, and to believe it without asking myself why . . . but most apt and most willing to be led by reason to any way or from it.

William Chillingworth

But ask not, to what doctors I apply?
Sworn to no master, of no sect am I:
As drives the storm, at any door I knock:
And house with Montaigne now, or now with Locke.

Pope

Knowledge and the Open Mind

In Athens where Books and Wits were ever busier than in any other part of Greece, I finde but only two sorts of writings which the magistrate car'd to take notice of: those either blasphemous and Atheisticall, or Libellous. Of other sects and opinions (though tending to voluptuousness and the denying of divine providence) they took no heed. Therefore we do not read that either Epicurus or that libertine school of Cyrene, or what the Cynick impudence utter'd, was ever questioned by the Laws. Neither is it recorded that the writings of those old comedians were suppress . . . and that Plato commended the reading of Aristophanes, the loosest of them all, to his royall scholler Dionysius is commonly known. . . .

God, though he commands us temperance, justice, continence,

yet pours out before us ev'n to a profusion all desirable things and gives us minds that can wander beyond all limit and satiety. Why should we then affect a rigor contrary to the manner of God and of nature by abridging or scanting those means, which books, freely permitted, are, both to the trial of virtue and the exercise of truth. ... We must not think to make a staple commodity of all the knowledge in the Land, to mark and licence it like our broad-cloth and our wooll packs. ... I could recount what I have seen and heard in other Countries, where this kind of inquisition tyrannizes; when I have sat among their learned men ... and bin counted happy to be born in such a place of Philosophic freedom as they suppos'd England were. ... There it was that I found and visited the famous Galileo grown old, a prisoner to the Inquisition, for thinking in Astronomy otherwise than the Franciscan and Dominican licencers thought.

John Milton: *Areopagitica*

Dislike of the unfamiliar

Since the time of Carlyle, "earnestness" has been a favourite virtue in literature, and it is customary to treat this wish to twist other people's belief into ours as if it were a part of the love of truth. But the mass of mankind have ... no such fine motive. Independently of truth or falsehood, the spectacle of a different belief from ours is disagreeable to us, in the same way that the spectacle of a different form of dress and manners is disagreeable. A set of schoolboys will persecute a new boy with a new sort of jacket: they will hardly let him have a new-shaped penknife. Grown up people are just as bad, except when culture has softened them ... much of the feeling of "earnest believers" is I believe altogether the same. They wish others to think as they do, not only because they wish to diffuse truth, but also and much more because they cannot bear to hear the words of a creed different from their own.

Walter Bagehot

The necessity of variety of opinion

Where there is much desire to learn, there of necessity will be much arguing, much writing, many opinions, for opinion in good men is but knowledge in the making . . . and when every stone is laid artfully together, it cannot be united into a continuity, it can but be contiguous in this world; neither can every peece of the building be of one form; nay, rather the perfection consists in this: that out of many moderat varieties and brotherly dissimilitudes that are not vastly disproportionall arises the goodly and the gracefull symmetry that commends the whole pile and structure.

John Milton: *Areopagitica*

JESUS . . . for the satisfaction of your longing for the truth I will tell you that the answer to your demand is your own argument that neither you nor the prisoner whom you judge can prove that he is in the right; therefore you must not judge me lest you be yourself judged. Without sedition and blasphemy the world would stand still and the kingdom of God never be a stage nearer. . . .

PILATE And I am to spare and encourage every heretic, every rebel, every lawbreaker, every rapscallion lest he should turn out to be wiser than all the generations who made the Roman law and built up the Roman Empire on it?

JESUS By their fruits ye shall know them. Beware how you kill a thought that is new to you. For that thought may be the foundation of the kingdom of God on earth. . . .

PILATE . . . You are a more dangerous fellow than I thought. For your blasphemy against the god of the high priests I care nothing: you may trample their religion into hell for all I care; but you have blasphemed against Caesar and against the Empire; and you mean it, and have the power to turn men's hearts against it as you have half turned mine. Therefore I must make an end of you whilst there is still some law left in the world.

JESUS Law is blind without counsel. . . . Slay me and you go blind to your damnation. The greatest of God's names is Counsellor; and when your Empire is dust and your name a byword among the nations the temples of the living God shall still ring with his praise as Wonderful! Counsellor! the Everlasting Father, the Prince of Peace.

And so the last word remains with Christ and Handel; and this must stand as the best defence of Tolerance until a better man than I makes a better job of it.

George Bernard Shaw: Preface to *On the Rocks*

We are constantly struck in the Encyclopaedia by a genuine desire to reach the best opinion by the only right way, the way of abundant many-sided and liberal discussion. . . . The Encyclopaedists were the most ardent propagators of the modern principle of tolerance. No one has to be reminded that this was something more than an abstract discussion among the doctors of social philosophy in a country where youths were broken on the wheel for levity in face of an ecclesiastical procession, where nearly every considerable man of the century had been either banished or imprisoned for daring to use his mind and which had been half ruined by the great proscription of Protestants more than once renewed. The article Tolerance was greatly admired in its day and it is an eloquent and earnest reproduction of the pleas of Locke.

Diderot himself in an earlier article (Intolérance) had treated the subject with more than trenchant energy. . . . He winds up with a description of the intolerant as one who forgets that a man is his fellow, . . . as a man to whom it comes easier to have zeal than morals.

John Morley: *Diderot and the Encyclopaedists*

Boundless communication

Standing for truth means necessarily standing for all truth, not only for my glimpse of it. It is not only tolerance that ends where I insist, without further test, on my own truth against truth from other quarters . . . it is truth itself that ends, for it becomes a merely subjective estimate of what is true for myself unless I try incessantly to widen it by listening to and comparing the convictions of my fellow men with my own.

. . . Boundless communication must not be mistaken for accepting supinely everything as true that comes my way. The very process of exchange includes an active concern for sifting and discerning truth from falsehood. But this happens only through the living struggle for greater truth on the battlefield of tolerance. Indeed, just because more truth can be found only in boundless communication, it is through tolerance, which alone makes such communication possible, that truth is stood for and falsehood defied. A genuine stand for truth is not made by the intolerance of falsehood, but only by enlarging truth through tolerance.

Richard K. Ullmann: *Tolerance and the Intolerable*

Liberty not to be feared

And let him be Jew, or Papist, or Turk, or Heathen, or Protestant, or what sort soever, or such as worship sun or moon or sticks or stones, let them have liberty where every one may bring forth his strength, and have free liberty to speak forth his mind and judgment. For the ministers of the gospel, who have the spiritual weapons, need not fear none of them all; for they have the shield of faith, the armour of light, and the breastplate of righteousness; they are armed soldiers with spiritual weapons, and they need not cry out to the magistrates.

George Fox: *Doctrinals*

Each little sect or religion has doubtless had some germ of the truth within it, which has rendered it subservient to the great purpose of fertilizing the world—but so long as the professors of either of them think that they are favoured Children of the Divine

Father, whom He regards with a complacency with which He does not view the rest of Humanity, so long is the fulness of God's idea not attained by them.

Let it not be objected that speculations upon the mysteries of religion are forbidden . . . the development of revealed truths into truths of reason is absolutely necessary, if the human race is to be helped by them. When they were revealed they were certainly no truths of reason, but they were revealed in order to become such. They were like the "that makes" of the mathematical master, which he says to the boys beforehand, in order to partly direct them in their reckoning. If the scholars were to be satisfied with the "that makes", they would never learn to calculate. . . . It is not true that speculations upon these things have ever done harm. . . . You must find fault, not with the speculations but with the folly and the tyranny of checking them. You must lay the blame on those who would not permit men, having their own speculations, to indulge in them.

Lessing: *The Education of the Human Race*
(trans. F. W. Robertson)

(King Utopus) hearing that the inhabitants of the land were, before his coming thither, at continual dissension and strife among themselves for their religions; perceiving also that this common dissension (whilest every several sect took several parts in fighting for their country) was the only occasion of his conquest over them all; as soon as he had gotten the victory, first of all he made a decree, that it should bc lawful for every man to favour and follow what religion he would, and that he might do the best he could to bring other to his opinion, so that he did it peaceably, gently, quietly and soberly, without hasty and contentious rebuking and inveighing against other. . . . This law did King Utopus make not only for the maintenance of peace, which he saw through continual contention and mortal hatred utterly extinguished; but also because he thought this decree should make for the furtherance of religion. Whereof he durst define and determine nothing unadvisedly, as doubting whether God, desiring manifold and diverse sorts of honour, would inspire sundry men with sundry kinds of religion. And this surely he thought a very unmeet and foolish thing, and a point of arrogant presumption, to compel all other by violence and threatenings to agree to the same that thou believest to be true. Furthermore though there be one religion which alone is true, and all other vain and superstitious, yet did he well foresee (so that the matter were handled with reason, and sober modesty) that the truth, of (its) own power, would at the last issue out and come to light. But if contention and debate in that behalf should continually be used, as the worst men be most obstinate and stubborn, and in their evil opinion most constant; he perceived that then the best and holiest religion would be trodden underfoot and destroyed by most vain superstitions, even as good corn is by thorns and weeds overgrown and choked. Therefore all this matter he left undiscussed, and gave to every man free liberty and chance to believe what he would. . . . Nothing is heard or seen in the churches, but that which seemeth to agree indifferently with all (religious creeds). If there be a distinct kind of sacrifice peculiar to any several sects, that they execute at home in their own houses. The public sacrifices be so ordered, that they be no derogation nor prejudice to any of the private sacrifices and religions. Therefore no image of any god is seen in the church, to the intent that it may be free for every man to conceive God, by his own religion, after what likeness and similitude he will.

Sir Thomas More: *Utopia*

In formal logic, a contradiction is the signal of a defeat: but in the evolution of real knowledge it marks the first step in progress towards a victory. This is one great reason for the utmost toleration of variety of opinion. Once and for ever, this duty of toleration has been summed up in the words, "Let both grow together until the harvest". The failure of Christians to act up to this precept, of the highest authority, is one of the curiosities of religious history. But we have not yet exhausted the discussion of the moral temper required for the pursuit of truth. There are short cuts leading merely to an illusory success. It is easy enough to find a theory, logically harmonious and with important applications in the region of fact, provided that you are content to disregard half your evidence. Every age produces people with clear logical intellects, and with the most praiseworthy grasp of the importance of some sphere of human experience, who have elaborated, or inherited, a scheme of thought which exactly fits those experiences which claim their interest. Such people are apt resolutely to ignore, or to explain away, all evidence which confuses their scheme with contradictory instances. What they cannot fit in is for them nonsense. An unflinching determination to take the whole evidence into account is the only method of preservation against the fluctuating extremes of fashionable opinion. This advice seems so easy, and is in fact so difficult to follow.

Alfred North Whitehead: *Science and the Modern World*

Obsession is the key to the tragedies of history. Apprehension of one truth so vivid as to make it appear as the whole and final truth is such an obsession. And round the luminous spot where the mind is focussed there presently gathers a cloud of phantasies.

Lionel Curtis: *Civitas Dei*

I say that the State power should not be used to arrest discussion because the State power may be used equally for truth or error, . . . but in discussion truth has an advantage. . . . If you let the human mind alone, it has a preference for good argument over bad . . . but if you do not let it alone, you substitute a game of force, where all doctrines are equal, for a game of logic, where the truer have the better chance. . . . [It is true that] there were unhappy ages before Liberty and Toleration became possible. . . . The case is analogous to that of education . . . the restrictions that are useful at nine years old are pernicious at nineteen . . . but there are many most able persons who turn the matter just the other way. . . . They say, "I would no sooner let the nation at large read that bad book than I would let my children read it". At heart they think that they are wiser than the mass of mankind, just as they are wiser than their children, and would regulate the studies of both unhesitatingly . . . and the best is that the minds of most would be persecutors are themselves unfixed; their opinions are in a perpetual flux; they would persecute all others for tenets which yesterday they had not heard of and which they will not believe tomorrow. . . . Without discussion each mind is dependent on its own partial observation. . . . To prohibit discussion is to prohibit the corrective process.

Walter Bagehot

How many other things might be tolerated in peace and left to conscience, had we but charity, and were it not the chief strong hold of our hypocrisie to be ever judging one another. I fear yet this iron yoke of outward conformity hath left a slavish print upon our necks; the ghost of a linnen decency yet haunts us. We stumble and are impatient at the least dividing of one visible congregation from another, though it be not in fundamentalls; and through our forwardnes to suppresse, and our backwardnes to recover any enthrall'd peece of truth out of the gripe of custom, we care not to keep truth separated from truth, which is the fiercest rent and disunion of all. We doe not see that while we still affect by all means a rigid externall formality, we may as soon fall again into a grosse conforming stupidity, a stark and dead congealment of wood and hay and stubble forc't and frozen together. . . . Not that I can think well of every light separation, or that all in a Church is to be expected gold and silver and pretious stones; it is not possible for man to sever the wheat from the tares, the good fish from the other frie; that must be the Angels Ministery at the end of mortall things. Yet if all cannot be of one mind, as who looks they should be? this doubtles is more wholsome, more prudent, and more Christian: that many be tolerated rather than all compell'd.

John Milton: *Areopagitica*

I was called one afternoon to the telephone (not knowing anything about the controversy) to talk with the representative of one of our most distinguished morning papers . . . The Voice said: "What do you use for the plural of Rhinoceros?"

"Rhinoceroses," said I, "almost the only remaining beauty I was taught in childhood."

"You don't say 'Rhinos'," asked the Voice.

"Only in limericks," said I.

"The feet of your favourite Rhino
  Are apt to leave marks on the lino,
  But if you—"

"You think," the Voice interrupted, "that yours is the *right* plural?"

"Certainly not," said I, "the Oxford Dictionary gives six or seven, rhinoceron among others, a charming word."

"Yes, we have those," the Voice said warmly, "but which of them is *right*?"

"All," I answered tenderly, "it is why they are there."

"But," the Voice went on, or words to this effect, "there needs must be some one Best way of worship. One nobler than the rest. Which is *right*. Rhinoceroses take so *long*."

My mind reverted to English verse, to the dance of five syllables in the time of two, to all lovely freedom in law, to the joy of six possibilities, to variation, man's continual delight. I said passionately: "You could say it in almost the same time. Must you dragoon us? Must you forbid the Rhinoceros to broaden slowly down?. . ."

Charles Williams: *The Image of the City*

I know the general cavill against general learning is this . . . He that sips of many arts, drinks of none. However we must know, that all learning, which is but one grand Science, hath so homogeneall a body, that the parts thereof do with a mutuall service relate to, and communicate strength and lustre each to other. . . . Thus taking these Sciences in their general latitude he hath finished the round circle or golden ring of the arts; only he keeps a place for the diamond to be set in, I mean for that predominant profession of Law, Physick, Divinitie or State policie which he intends for his principall calling hereafter.

Thomas Fuller

To a person uninstructed in natural history, his country or sea-side stroll is a walk through a gallery filled with wonderful works of art, nine-tenths of which have their faces turned to the wall. Teach him something of natural history, and you place in his hands a catalogue of those which are worth turning round. Surely our innocent pleasures are not so abundant in this life that we can afford to despise this or any other source of them. We should fear being banished for our neglect to that limbo, where the great Florentine tells us are those who during this life "wept when they might be joyful".

Thomas Huxley: *Essays*

Nature, so far as in her lies,
Imitates God, and turns her face
To every land beneath the skies,
Counts nothing that she meets with base
But lives and loves in every place.

Tennyson

I hold there is a general beauty in the works of God, and therefore no deformity in any kind or species of creature whatsoever. I cannot tell by what logic we call a toad, a bear, or an elephant ugly, they being created in those outward shapes and figures which best express those actions of their inward forms. And having passed that general visitation of God, who saw that all that he had made was good, that is, conformable to his will, which abhors deformity, and is the rule of order and beauty; there is no deformity but in monstrosity, wherein notwithstanding there is a kind of beauty. Nature so ingeniously contriving the irregular parts, as they become sometimes more remarkable than the principal fabric.

Sir Thomas Browne: *Religio Medici*

You've seen the world—
The beauty and the wonder and the power
The shapes of things, their colours, lights and shades,
Changes, surprises—and God made it all!
For what? . . .—What's it all about?
To be passed over, despised? or dwelt upon,
Wondered at? Oh, this last of course—you say.
But why not do as well as say, paint these
Just as they are, careless of what comes of it?
God's works—paint any one, and count it crime
To let a truth slip.

Browning: *Fra Lippo Lippi*

Pierre Leroy said of Pierre Teilhard de Chardin that there was only "one limit to his tolerance: the one fault he detested" was any sort of 'disgust with life'. "May the Lord only preserve in me," he wrote, "a passionate taste for the world, and a great gentleness, and may He help me to persevere to the end in the fullness of humanity."

Pierre Teilhard de Chardin: *Letters from a Traveller*

No business serious seemed but one; no work
But one was found; and that did in me live.
D'ye ask me what? It was with clearer eyes
To see all creatures full of Deities;
Especially one's self: And to admire
The satisfaction of all true desire:

T'was to be pleased with all that God hath done;
T'was to enjoy even all beneath the sun:
T'was with a steady and immediate sense
To feel and measure all the excellence
Of things; t'was to inherit endless treasure,
And to be filled with everlasting pleasure:

*

To prize and to be ravish'd; to be true
Sincere and single in a blessed view
Of all His gifts.

Traherne

"Dans littérature," said M. Taine, "j'aime tout." I would shake his hand for saying that and add: "In life, Monsieur, as well." All things attract me equally. I am ready to do anything, go anywhere, think anything, read anything. Wherever I hitch my waggon I am confident of an adventurous ride . . . I will go with you to Norway, Switzerland, Jericho, Timbuctoo. Talk to me about the Rosicrucians or the stomach of a flea and I will listen to you. Tell me that the Chelsea Power Station is as beautiful as the Parthenon at Athens and I'll believe you. Everything is beautiful, even the ugly—why did Whistler paint the squalor of the London streets, or Brangwyn the gloom of a steam-crane?

"The works of man don't interest me much," an enthusiast in Natural History once said to me, "I prefer the works of God." . . . He was one of those forlorn creatures with a carefully ordered mind, his information and opinions written out in indelible ink, and pigeon-holed for easy reference . . . He never shuddered to reflect upon the limitations of a single point of view—other folk were simply *wrong*. He was scarcely one to understand the magnanimous phrase of the French, "Tout comprendre c'est tout pardonner". Other folk were either good or bad.

W. N. P. Barbellion: *Enjoying Life*

What more felicity can fall to creature
Than to enjoy delight with liberty
And to be lord of all the works of nature,
To range in th'air from th'earth to highest sky,
To feed on flowers and weeds of glorious feature,
To take whatever thing doth please the eye?
Who rests not pleased with such happiness,
Well worthy he to taste of wretchedness.

Spenser

To obtain the greatest and most worthy pleasure out of your few years of life it is essential that you should have so trained your faculties as to take an interest in, and pleasure in, the most various matters, in everything in fact around you, and even in many things far off and inaccessible.

Sir Alexander Kennedy

For my part I could never think any part of Learning either useless or contemptible, because I knew not the Advantages of it; I have rather thought myself obliged to reverence those who are skilful in any Art or Profession, and can gladly subscribe to the Praise of any Liberal Accomplishment, be it in any Person, of any Sex.

Elizabeth Elstob: Preface to *Homily on the birth of St. Gregory*

II

The Search for Truth—Looking to the Future

New opinions are always suspended and usually opposed without any other reason, but because they are not already common.

Locke

If we really admire one another, we bring, drunken with the world and with ourselves, the hearts of new men into the ancient universe.

Baudelaire

LORD SUMMERHAYES: I should keep an open mind about it.

JOHNNY: Has it ever occurred to you that a man with an open mind must be a bit of a scoundrel? If you ask me I like a man who makes up his mind once and for all as to what's right and what's wrong and then sticks to it. At all events you know where to have him.

BENTLEY: He may want to have you, old chap.

JOHNNY: Well, let him . . . An open mind is all very well in clever talky-talky; but in conduct and in business, give me solid ground.

LORD SUMMERHAYES: Yes: the quicksands make life difficult. Still, there they are. It's no use pretending they're rocks.

JOHNNY: I don't know. You can draw a line and make other chaps toe it. That's what I call morality.

LORD SUMMERHAYES: Very true. But you don't make any progress when you're toeing a line.

G. B. Shaw: *Misalliance*

The man who is certain he is right is almost sure to be wrong, and he has the additional misfortune of inevitably remaining so. All our theories are fixed upon uncertain data, and all of them want alteration and support. Ever since the world began opinion has changed with the progress of things; and it is something more than absurd to suppose that we have a sure claim to perfection, or that we are in possession of the highest stretch of intellect which has resulted or can result from human thought. Why our successors should not displace us in our opinions, as well as our persons, it is difficult to say; it has ever been so, and from analogy would be supposed to continue so; and yet, with all this practical evidence of the fallibility of our opinions, all, and none more than philosophers, are ready to assert the real truth of their opinions.

Michael Faraday: *On the Forms of Matter*

[Berengarius of Tours, scholastic theologian, was accused of heresy. He repeatedly abjured but never wholly abandoned his beliefs.]

No more 'twixt conscience staggering and the Pope
Soon shall I now before my God appear,
By him to be acquitted, as I hope;
By him to be condemned, as I fear.—

(*Reflection on the above*)
Lynx amid moles! had I stood by thy bed,
Be of good cheer, meek soul! I would have said:
I see a hope spring from that humble fear.
All are not strong alike through storms to steer
Right onward. What? though dread of threatened death
And dungeon torture made thy hand and breath
Inconstant to the truth within thy heart?

*

Ye, who secure mid trophies not your own
Judge him who won them when he stood alone
And proudly talk of recreant Berengare—
O first the age, and then the man compare!
That age how dark! congenial minds how rare!
No host of friends with kindred zeal did burn!
No throbbing hearts awaited his return!
Prostrate alike when prince and peasant fell,
He only disenchanted from the spell,
Like the weak worm that gems the starless night
Moved in the scanty circlet of his light;
And was it strange if he withdrew the ray
That did but guide the night-birds to their prey?
The ascending Day-star with a bolder eye
Hath lit each dewdrop on our trimmer lawn!
Yet not for this, if wise, will we decry
The spots and struggles of the timid Dawn;

Lest so we tempt th'approaching Noon to scorn
The mists and painted vapours of our Morn.

S. T. Coleridge: *Lines suggested by the last work of Berengarius, Ob. Anno Dom. 1088*

In an intellectual age there can be no active interest which puts aside all hope of a vision of the harmony of truth. To acquiesce in discrepancy is destructive of candour, and of moral cleanliness. It belongs to the self-respect of intellect to pursue every tangle of thought to its final unravelment. If you check that impulse, you will get no religion and no science from an awakened thoughtfulness. The important question is, In what spirit are we going to face the issue? There we come to something absolutely vital.

A clash of doctrines is not a disaster—it is an opportunity. I will explain my meaning by some illustrations from science. The weight of an atom of nitrogen was well known. Also it was an established scientific doctrine that the average weight of such atoms in any considerable mass will be always the same. Two experimenters, the late Lord Rayleigh and the late Sir William Ramsay, found that if they obtained nitrogen by two different methods, each equally effective for that purpose, they always observed a persistent slight difference between the average weights of the atoms in the two cases. Now I ask you, would it have been rational of these men to have despaired because of this conflict between chemical theory and scientific observation? . . . What Rayleigh and Ramsay did was this: They at once perceived that they had hit upon a line of investigation which would disclose some subtlety of chemical theory that had hitherto eluded observation. The discrepancy was not a disaster: it was an opportunity to increase the sweep of chemical knowledge. You all know the end of the story: finally argon was discovered, a new chemical element which had lurked undetected, mixed with the nitrogen. . . . Further researches of the most careful accuracy were undertaken. . . . The research has effected a great stride in the power of chemical theory, far transcending in importance the discovery of argon from which it originated. The moral of these stories lies on the surface, and I will leave to you their application to the case of religion and science.

Alfred North Whitehead: *Science and the Modern World*

Knowledge and power have rights,
But ignorance and weakness have rights too.
There needs no crucial effort to find truth
If here or there or anywhere about:
We ought to turn each side, try hard and see,
And if we can't, be glad we've earned at least
The right, by one laborious proof the more,
To graze in peace earth's pleasant pasturage.
Men are not angels, neither are they brutes:
Something we may see, all we cannot see.

Browning: *Bishop Blougram's Apology*

Perceptions of beauty have an infinite complexity: they are all subtle aggregates of countless details, and about each of these details probably every mind in some degree differs from every other one. ... Each mind which is true to itself, and which draws its own impressions carefully, and which compares those impressions with the impressions of others arrives at certain conclusions, which as far as that mind is concerned are ultimate. These it sets down or communicates by word of mouth, and these again form data which other minds can contrast with their own. In this incessant comparison eccentric minds fall off on every side. ... Each epoch has its violent partisans, who will listen to nothing else. ... These violent minds are always faulty and sometimes absurd, but they are almost always useful to mankind. Most useful, too, are others less apparent; shrinking, sensitive, testing minds. The human mind of a certain maturity, *if left alone*, prefers real beauty to sham beauty, and prefers it the sooner if original men suggest new charms, and quiet men criticize and judge of them. But an aesthetical persecution would derange all this, for generally the compulsive power would be in the hands of the believers in some tradition. . . . But it will be said, 'Whoever heard of such nonsense as an aesthetical persecution?' . . . [But] the case of morals and religion in which people have always persecuted and still wish to persecute is the very same. If there are (as I myself think there are) ultimate truths of morals and religion which more or less vary for each mind the comparison of one mind with another is necessary; the same discussion; the same use of criticising minds; the same use of original ones. The mode of arriving at truth is the same and also the mode of stopping it. . . . You may prevent the admirers of Claude from seeing his pictures or from praising them; but you cannot make them admirers of Turner. Just so you may by persecution prevent minds prone to be Protestant from being Protestant; but you will not make men real Catholics . . . you will make of them, instead, more or less conscious sceptics.

Persecution in intellectual countries produces a superficial conformity, but also underneath an intense, incessant, implacable doubt.

Walter Bagehot

Meanwhile materialism denies humanity in which the religious sense, like the artistic and philosophical, is an alienable element of life: it denies tradition—the harmony of which with the voice of individual inspiration and conscience is the sole criterion of truth we possess on earth; it denies history, which teaches us that religions are transitory, but Religion is eternal; it denies the solemn witness borne in adoration of God and the Ideal, by a long series of our greatest minds . . . it denies the power of revelation innate in man, in order to date the discovery of truth from the meagre labours upon a fragment of creation studied by one single faculty of the mind.

Mazzini: *A letter to the Members of the Œcumenical Council*

The present must not attempt to schoolmaster the future by pretending to know good from evil in tendency, or protect citizens against shocks to their opinions and convictions, moral, political, or religious: in other words it must not persecute doctrines of any kind, or what is called bad taste, and must insist on all persons facing such shocks as they face frosty weather or any of the other disagreeable, dangerous, or bracing incidents of freedom. The expediency of Toleration has been forced on us by the fact that progressive enlightenment depends on a fair hearing for doctrines which at first appear seditious, blasphemous, and immoral, and which deeply shock people who never think originally, thought being with them merely a habit and an echo. The deeper ground for Toleration is the nature of creation, which, as we now know, proceeds by evolution. Evolution finds its way by experiment; and this finding of the way varies according to the stage of development reached, from the blindest groping along the line of least resistance to conscious intellectual speculation, with its routine of hypothesis and verification, induction and deduction; or even into so rapid and intuitive an integration of all these processes in a single brain that we get the inspired guess of the man of genius and the fanatical resolution of the teacher of new truths who is first slain as a blasphemous apostate and then worshipped as a prophet.

G. B. Shaw: Preface to Parents and Children (*Misalliance*)

Religion will not regain its old power until it can face change in the same spirit as does science. Its principles may be eternal, but the expression of those principles requires continual development. This evolution of religion is in the main a disengagement of its own proper ideas from the adventitious notions which have crept into it by reason of the expression of its own ideas in terms of the imaginative picture of the world entertained in previous ages. . . .

The religious controversies of the sixteenth and seventeenth centuries put theologians into a most unfortunate state of mind. They were always attacking and defending. They pictured themselves as the garrison of a fort surrounded by hostile forces. All such pictures express half-truths. That is why they are so popular. But they are dangerous. This particular picture fostered a pugnacious party spirit which really expresses an ultimate lack of faith. They dared not modify, because they shirked the task of disengaging their spiritual message from the associations of a particular imagery. ... The worship of God is not a rule of safety—it is an adventure of the spirit, a flight after the unattainable. The death of religion comes with the repression of the high hope of adventure.

Alfred North Whitehead: *Science and the Modern World*

I have felt a tenderness in my mind towards persons in two circumstances ... namely, towards such active members (of the Society of Friends) as keep slaves and such as hold offices in civil government; and I have desired that Friends, in all their conduct, may be kindly affectioned one towards another. Many Friends who keep slaves ... at times think about trying them with freedom, but find many things in their way. The way of living and the diurnal expenses of some of them are such that it seems impracticable for them to set their slaves free without changing their own way of life. ... Whatever a man does in the spirit of charity, to him it is not sin ... Yet others, who live in the same spirit of charity, from a clear convincement may see the relation of one thing to another.

In the history of the reformation from Popery it is observable that the progress was gradual from age to age. The uprightness of the first reformers in attending to the light and understanding given to them opened the way for sincere-hearted people to proceed further afterwards; and thus each one truly fearing God and labouring in the works of righteousness appointed for him in his day findeth acceptance with Him.

Deeprooted customs, though wrong, are not easily altered; but it is the duty of every man to be firm in that which he certainly knows is right for him.

John Woolman

It must be borne in mind that to proceed gradually is the law of life in all its expressions; therefore in human institutions, too, it is not possible to renovate for the better except by working from within them, gradually. Pius XII proclaimed: "Salvation and justice are not to be found in revolution, but in evolution through concord. Violence has always achieved only destruction, not construction; the kindling of passions, not their pacification; the accumulation of hate and ruin, not the reconciliation of the contending parties. And it has reduced men and parties to the difficult task of rebuilding, after sad experience, on the ruins of discord".

Pope John XXIII: *Pacem in Terris*

Think not that, in objecting to the opinions of certain classes of Christians, I divest myself of christian charity. True charity consists in wishing well to all persons, in doing them every kind office in our power, and thinking as well of them as we can. And certainly the greatest errors in judgment are consistent with the best dispositions, and consequently with the most perfect acceptableness with God, who looks only to the heart and to the opportunities which he has afforded to every man for the discovery of truth.

A love of truth is an essential part of a good moral character, and consequently an earnest endeavour to divest ourselves of every prejudice in our search after it. They, therefore, who are either negligent in their own enquiries, or who in any degree persecute others, on account of their difference of opinion, are highly censurable. But such is the force of prejudice, especially in favour of opinions in the belief of which men have been educated, and which they have long held sacred, that the greatest allowance is to be made even for their undue attachment to them, and for every natural consequence of that attachment. At the same time, therefore, that I regard with horror such doctrines as those of transubstantiation, the trinity, atonement, and other corruptions of Christianity . . . I regard the *men* who hold them with the greatest respect, and entertain for them the greatest good will. Though they differ so much from me, they may be greatly my superiors both in understanding and in piety.

Joseph Priestley: *Tracts relating to the Dissenters*

Sooner or later the unification of the human race is bound to come, and if the world wishes to survive there must be an end to racial conflict. For its maturity the earth needs every drop of its blood.

Pierre Teilhard de Chardin: *Letters from a Traveller*

At the date of Galileo's controversy with the Inquisition, Galileo's way of stating the facts was, beyond question, the fruitful procedure for the sake of scientific research. But in itself it was not more true than the formulation of the Inquisition. But at that time the modern concepts of relative motion were in nobody's mind; so that the statements were made in ignorance of the qualifications required for their more perfect truth. Yet this question of the motions of the earth and the sun expresses a real fact in the universe; and all sides had got hold of important truths concerning it. But with the knowledge of those times, the truths appeared to be inconsistent.

Again I will give you another example taken from the state of modern physical science. Since the time of Newton and Huyghens in the seventeenth century there have been two theories as to the physical nature of light.... The two theories are contradictory. In the eighteenth century Newton's theory was believed, in the nineteenth century Huyghens' theory was believed.... Scientists have to leave it at that, and wait for the future, in the hope of attaining some wider vision which reconciles both.

We should apply these same principles to the questions in which there is a variance between science and religion. We would believe nothing in either sphere of thought which does not appear to us to be certified by solid reasons based upon the critical research either of ourselves or of competent authorities. But granting that we have honestly taken this precaution, a clash between the two on points of detail where they overlap should not lead us hastily to abandon doctrines for which we have solid evidence. It may be that we are more interested in one set of doctrines than in the other. But, if we have any sense of perspective and of the history of thought, we shall wait and refrain from mutual anathemas.

We should wait: but we should not wait passively, or in despair. The clash is a sign that there are wider truths and finer perspectives within which a reconciliation of a deeper religion and a more subtle science will be found.

Alfred North Whitehead: *Science and the Modern World*

A Sicilian peasant discovers growth through tolerance

CICCIO Supposing you meet some of the men, or even the women, in the neighbourhood and get talking and one of them says to you, "You're wrong", you shouldn't go off the handle at once and answer "Mind your own business". You should think over what he's said and ask yourself: "Am I really wrong?" And reflect well before telling him to go to the devil. There is none of this sort of give-and-take among equals here. Whereas if a man were to think about what he saw in his relations with others, he could make his own personal apostleship even when he was working in the fields and learn ever so many things about life. Thinking about things can lead to change. "Wouldn't it be better to do it like this or do it like that?" one wonders —and lo and behold, one gets a new idea, a sudden inspiration.

DANILO When you speak of apostleship just what do you mean?

CICCIO "Apostleship" is really just a word I've used . . . meaning, let's say, something like "founded on" . . . you, for example, you have an apostleship. An apostleship, for me, is like this: a person, who has an idea, a vocation, a mission, setting out to teach others the right road in life. This is apostleship to my way of thinking.

DANILO In my case, however, I am asking others to help me find the right road. It's not that I have the truth neatly folded up in my trouser pocket all ready to be pulled out and taught to others.

CICCIO That's true, but you are one who seeks the truth and can lead others to seek it, too. That's why it is that those who come to knowledge can lead others to seek it also.

DANILO In other words, those who do not seek do not find.

Danilo Dolci: *Waste*

Then loudly cried the bold Sir Bedivere,
"Ah! my Lord Arthur, whither shall I go?

*

For now I see the true old times are dead,
When every morning brought a noble chance,
And every chance brought out a noble knight.

*

But now the whole Round Table is dissolved
Which was an image of the mighty world;
And I, the last, go forth companionless.
And the days darken round me, and the years,
Among new men, strange faces, other minds."

And slowly answer'd Arthur from the barge;
"The old order changeth, yielding place to new,
And God fulfils himself in many ways
Lest one good custom should corrupt the world."

Alfred Tennyson: *Morte D'Arthur*

What I want to do, in short, is to express the psychology of the man who sees himself no longer as a Frenchman, or a Chinaman but as a terrestrial. The further I go the more determined I become to live above political and national prejudices of any sort, and to say openly what I think. . . . I believe that the time has come when, if men are ever to achieve a common understanding, they must do so at a point which will be reached only be breaking, reversing or reframing a mass of conventions and prejudices that enclose us in a dead outer shell.

Pierre Teilhard de Chardin: *Letters from a Traveller*

In the first opening of the Wars—the Wars of Religion in Germany and France, of Revolt in the Netherlands, of the wars between Spain and England, of the Thirty Years War in the Empire, and the lesser but related crises in Scotland, in Scandinavia, in

Switzerland—there was everywhere a belief in and hope for ultimate military and metaphysical victory. That hope and belief were soon complicated by other causes, social and economic; and as in the Netherlands, Catholics and Calvinists sometimes found themselves strange tent-fellows and treaty-fellows. Economics confused the process of the Reformation as they had been partly responsible for the beginning of the Reformation. But the general dreams of things to come were still dictated by the subconscious habits of a thousand years. . . . Compromise was unthinkable, and toleration had to be a necessity before it could be a virtue. In fact, as a virtue it does not yet exist, though we once thought it did. For our fathers became bored and miserable and decadent through their incessant killing, and we, the children of that killing, supposed ourselves to be convinced of charity, when, in truth, we only shuddered still at the memory of blood.

Charles Williams: *The Descent of the Dove*

The price of progress

Man cannot live in community, as he is intended to live, unless the powers which he controls are offered to God and used for the benefit of his fellow men. Yet there are times . . . when human reason finds it well-nigh impossible to achieve community in this way, because it quite clearly sees that the thing cannot be done except at the price of such community as it has already achieved. And at that point human reason, for the most part says, "No", and holds what it has attained; and at that point the progress of man in community stops. He has refused the price of his true development, and sooner or later what he holds dear is destroyed.

. . . The whole of Christ's life had to do with this very thing. His temptations, His ministry, His Passion and His death were all because He saw the world as His Father's world and obeyed His Father's will, even to the giving back of His own most cherished inheritance as a son of Israel. For Christ gave back to God in Gethsemane the past and the future of his own people and his own heritage, in order that mankind might come into a new community.

R. F. Heath

III

The Fruits of the Open Mind

Reasonableness, Temperance, Balance, Discrimination

Let your moderation be known to all men.

Philippians

[The revised version reads "Let your *forbearance* be known to all men"; the New English Bible—"Let your *magnanimity* be known to all men". This threefold meaning of the Greek word επιείκεια is fully expressive of the spirit of tolerance.]

The longest Sword, the strongest Lungs, the most voices are false measures of Truth.

Benjamin Whichcote

The golden mean, and quiet flow
Of truths that soften hatred, temper strife.

Wordsworth

Mesure is medecyne . . .
For rightful reson shulde rule you alle
And kinde wit be Warden.

William Langland

The Light of Reason is calm and peaceable. Tis humen tranquillum et amicum; 'tis a Candle, not a Comet; it is a quiet and peaceable Light . . . the Lamp, 'tis only maintain'd with soft and peaceable Oyl. There is no jarring in pure Intellectuals; if men were tun'd and regulated by Reason more, there would be more Concord and Harmony in the World. As Man himself is a sociable Creature; so his Reason also is a sociable Light. This Candle would shine more clearly and equally, if the Windes of Passions were not injurious to it. T'were a commendable piece of Stoicism, if men could always hush and still those Waves that dash and beat against Reason. If they could scatter all those Clouds that soil and discolour the face and brightnesse of it: would there be such factions and commotions in the State; such Schisms and Ruptures in the Church; such hot and fiery persecutions of some trifling opinions? If the soft and sober voice of Reason were more attended to, Reason would make some differencies kiss and be friends, 'twould sheath up many a Sword, would quench many a flame, 'twould bind up many a Wound. This Candle of the Lord, 'twould scatter many a dark suspicion, many a sullen jealousie. Men may fall out in the dark sometimes, they cannot tell for what: if the Candle of the Lord were but amongst them, they would chide one another for nothing then but their former breaches.

Nathaniel Culverwel: *A Discourse of the Light of Nature*

Man comes into the world naked and unarmed, as if Nature had destined him for a social creature, and ordained that he should live under equitable laws and in peace, and as if she had desired that he should be guided by reason rather than driven by force.

William Harvey

The Rule of Right is the Reason of Things; the Judgment of Right is the Reason of our minds, perceiving the Reason of Things. To use Power, to controul the Principles of Human Nature; (the Use of Reason, the Exercise of Liberty) is as strange a Phenomenon, as to cross or pervert the common Course of Natural Agents; to bring the Sun back again, or to make it fill the world with darkness. God does not this: if he did, he would contest with himself; his Power would rise up against his Wisdom; and he would disparage and frustrate his own Workmanship. Why should We think to do that, which God will not do—to over-bear Reason with Violence!

Nathaniel Culverwel: *A Discourse of the Light of Nature*

Reason and love are the qualities which differentiate man from the beast, and the growth of their power is the only progress that matters in civilisation or in the individual. So far as man lives by them, he is fully human; so far as he departs from them, he is something less than his best self. But certainly love is no friend to intolerance, and the essence of tolerance is the belief that differences can and should be settled by reason, not by force, the belief that the victory of truth, though it may be slow in coming, is certain.

Sir Richard Livingstone: *Tolerance in Theory and Practice*

The meaning of sôphrosyné . . . is closely related to that old Greek rule of μηδὲν ἄγαν, nothing too much, which seems to us now rather commonplace, but has in its time stayed so many blind lusts and triumphant vengeances. It is something like Temperance, Gentleness, Mercy; sometimes Innocence, never mere Caution: a tempering of dominant emotions by gentler thought. But its derivation is interesting. The adjective σώφρων means "with saving thoughts". There is a way of thinking which destroys and a way which saves.

(*Rise of Greek Epic*)

Sôphrosyné, however we try to translate it, temperance, gentleness, the spirit that in any trouble thinks and is patient, that saves and not destroys, is the right spirit.

(*Four Stages of Greek Religion*)
Gilbert Murray

We should hardly think of the virtue of Temperance as specially characteristic of St. Paul, and even to the end of his days he probably found it difficult; yet in this he discovers the final proof of the working of Creative Spirit in his soul. He begins upon a note of convinced fervour: "The fruit—the harvest of the Spirit is love, joy, peace" . . . Then he pauses. We seem to see him thinking: "After all, I don't always feel like that. Things are often very trying. I don't seem able to love; peace and joy are unobtainable; I feel another law in my members warring against the law of my mind. Yet the indwelling Spirit is still there; to live *is* Christ. How does that Spirit act on my troubled spirit? . . . Surely in long-suffering, gentleness and kindness which I know must control all my reactions to the world of men." They were not the reactions which St. Paul found specially easy. . . . At last, at the very end, we reach those unexpected characters which are the earnest of his total transformation in the Spirit. Fidelity, Meekness, Moderation: an unsensational but unbroken loyalty to the infinite life and purpose which had made him its own, an acceptance of its gradual pace, a refusal to hurry, a restraining of the impetuous desire to get everything possible out of these new converts who were only babies still, and tell the candid truth to those who had let him down—these are the real fruits of his subjection to God. Paul, whose first idea had been to breathe fire and slaughter upon the Christians, and whose second idea had been to be "all out" for Christ . . . learns that the final gift of the Spirit is not intensity of life, but Temperance.

Evelyn Underhill: *The House of the Soul*

Thus, in the general rhythm of Christian life, development and renunciation, attachment and detachment, are not mutually exclusive. On the contrary, they harmonise, like breathing in and out in the movement of our lungs. They are two phases of the soul's breath, or two components of the impulse by which the Christian life uses things as a springboard from which to mount beyond them.

That is the general solution. In the detail of particular cases, the sequence of these two phases and the combinations of these two components are subject to an infinite number of subtle variations. Their exact blending calls for a spiritual tact which is the strength and virtue proper to the masters of the inner life. . . . It would clearly be as absurd to prescribe unlimited development or renunciation as it would be to set no bounds to eating or fasting. In the spiritual life, as in all organic processes, everyone has their optimum and it is just as harmful to go beyond it as not to attain it.

Pierre Teilhard de Chardin: *Le Milieu Divin*

[Moderation] is a mixture of discretion and charity in one's judgement. Yet such moderate men are commonly crushed betwixt the extreme parties on both sides. But what said Ignatius: "I am Christ's wheat and must be ground with the teeth of beasts, that I may be made God's pure manchet". Besides, in the world generally they get the least preferment; it faring with them as with the guest that sat in the midst of the table who could reach to neither messe, above or beneath him.

Pride is the greatest enemy to Moderation. This makes men stickle for their opinions, to make them fundamentall. Next to Pride—popular Applause is the greatest foe Moderation hath, and sure they who sail with that wind have their own vainglory for their Haven. To close up all, let men on God's blessing soundly, yet wisely, whip and lash Lukewarmnesse and Time-serving, their thongs will never flie in the face of true Moderation to do it any harm; for however men may undervalue it that Father [Ambrose] spake most truly, "Si virtutem finis ille fit maximas, qui plurimorum spectat profectum, Moderatio prope omnium pulcherrima est."

Thomas Fuller

... Our Trimmer is not eager to pick out the sore places in history against this or any other party; quite contrary, is very solicitous to find out anything that may be healing and tend to an agreement.... But mistakes, as all other things, have their periods, and many times the nearest way to cure is not to oppose them, but stay till they are trussed with their own weight. For Nature will not allow anything to continue long that is violent; violence is a wound, and a wound must be curable in a little time, or else it is mortal; but a nation cometh near being immortal, therefore the wound will one time or another be cured.

... Our Trimmer therefore, inspired by [the] Divine virtue [of truth] thinketh fit to conclude with these assertions—That our climate is a Trimmer between that part of the world where men are roasted, and the other where they are frozen; that our Church is a Trimmer between the frenzy of fanatic visions and the lethargic ignorance of Popish dreams; that our laws are Trimmers between the excesses of unbounded power and the extravagance of liberty not enough restrained; that true virtue hath ever been thought a Trimmer, and to have its dwelling in the middle between two extremes; and that even God Almighty Himself is divided between His two great attributes, His mercy and His justice.

Halifax: *Character of a Trimmer*

Avoid Extremes; and shun the fault of such,
Who still are pleas'd too little or too much.
At ev'ry trifle scorn to take offence,
That always shows great pride, or little sense;
Those heads, as stomachs, are not sure the best,
Which nauseate all, and nothing can digest.
... Some foreign writers, some our own despise:
The ancients only, or the Moderns prize.
Thus Wit, like Faith, by each man is apply'd
To one small sect, and all are damn'd beside.
Meanly they seek the blessing to confine
And force that sun but on a part to shine,

Which not alone the southern wit sublimes,
But ripens spirits in cold northern climes;
Which from the first has shone on ages past,
Enlights the present, and shall warm the last;
Tho' each may feel increases and decays
And see now clearer and now darker days.
Regard not then if Wit be old or new,
But blame the false, and value still the true.

Pope: *Essay on Criticism*

But what is the principle of tolerance? How should we define it? If I had to give a definition other than the unilluminating synonyms provided in dictionaries, I should borrow a term from Aristotle and say that tolerance is a mean between two extremes. The extremes are intolerance and indifference; on the one hand, "you *must* think and act as I do", on the other, "I couldn't care less". It is difficult to say which of these extremes is the worse.

Sir Richard Livingstone: *Tolerance in Theory and Practice*

To leave the mean is to abandon humanity. The greatness of the human soul consists in knowing how to preserve the mean. So far from greatness consisting in leaving it, it consists in not leaving it.

Pascal: *Pensées*

Man's great difficulty is to strive to walk through life, and through thought and practice in a straight line; to keep in medio—in that *golden mean*, which is our true centre of gravity and which we lost in Eden. We all tend like children, or the blind, the old, or the tipsy, to walk to one side, or wildly from one side to the other: one extreme breeds its opposite.

John Brown: *Horae Subsecivae*

Moderation is Wisdom

I think my conscience will not give me the lie, if I say there are not many extant that in a noble way fear the face of death less than myself; yet from the moral duty I owe to the commandment of God, and the natural respects that I tender unto the conservation of my essence and being, I would not perish upon a ceremony, politic points, or indifferency. Nor is my belief of that untractable temper, as not to bow at their obstacles, or connive at matters wherein there are not manifest impieties. The leaven, therefore, and ferment of all, not only civil, but religious actions, is wisdom; without which, to commit ourselves to the flames is homicide, and (I fear) but to pass through one fire into another.

Sir Thomas Browne: *Religio Medici*

This innocent word Trimmer signifieth no more than this, that if men are together in a boat, and one part of the company would weigh it down of one side, another would make it lean as much to the contrary; it happeneth there is a third opinion of those who conceive it would do as well if the boat went even, without endangering the passengers. Now it is hard to imagine . . . by what rule in sense this cometh to be a fault. . . . The dispute—which is the greater beauty, a monarchy or a commonwealth?—hath lasted long between their contending lovers; and they have behaved themselves too like lovers (who in good manners must be out of their wits) who have used such figures to exalt their own idol on either side or such angry aggravations to reproach one another in the contest that moderate men have in all times smiled upon this eagerness and thought it differed very little from a downright frenzy.

When all is done, those who look for perfection in this world may look as long as the Jews have done for their Messiah, therefore our Trimmer is not so unreasonably partial as to free our government from all objections. Our government is like our climate. There are winds which are sometimes loud and unquiet and yet with all the trouble they give us, we owe a great part of our health to them.

. . I will first lay this for a ground—that as there can be no true religion without charity, so there can be no true human prudence without bearing and condescention . . . moderate men will not be ready to involve a whole party in the guilt of a few [the Rye House Plot]. . . . Besides, men who act by a principle grounded upon moral virtue can never let it be entirely extinguished by the most repeated provocations. If a right thing, agreeable to Nature and good sense, taketh root in the heart of man that is impartial and unbiased, no outward circumstances can ever destroy it. . . . We may be taught, by the compassion that attendeth the most criminal men when they are condemned, that their faults are much more natural things than punishments; and that even the most necessary acts of severity do some kind of violence to our nature, whose indulgence will not be confined within the straight bounds of inexorable justice.

Halifax: *Character of a Trimmer*

A disentangled and a naked sense,
    A mind that's unpossest,
    A disengaged breast,
An empty and a quick intelligence
Acquainted with the golden mean,
An even spirit pure and serene,
Is that where beauty, excellence,
And pleasure keep their Court of Residence,
    My soul retire,
Get free, and so thou shalt even all admire.

Traherne

Comedy and Tolerance

And that the universe is just—or rather that it is not unjust, not malicious or cruel—is a fundamental assumption in Comedy. We must either believe that, or forget that we believe the opposite. More, it must be courteous, it must be willing to waive its rights.

Charles Williams: *The English Poetic Mind*

You may estimate your capacity for Comic perception by being able to detect the ridicule of them you love, without loving them less: and more by being able to see yourself somewhat ridiculous in dear eyes, and accepting the correction their image of you proposes. . . . If you detect the ridicule, and your kindliness is chilled by it, you are slipping into the grasp of Satire. You must, as I have said, believe that our state of society is founded in common-sense, otherwise you will not be struck by the contrasts the Comic Spirit perceives, or have it to look to for your consolation. You will, in fact, be standing in that peculiar oblique beam of light, yourself illuminated to the general eye as the very object of chase and doomed quarry of the thing obscure to you. . . . But to feel its presence and to see it, is your assurance that many sane and solid minds are with you in what you are experiencing: and this of itself spares you the pain of satirical heat, and the bitter craving to strike heavy blows. You share the sublime of wrath, that would not have hurt the foolish, but merely demonstrate their foolishness.

George Meredith: *Essay on Comedy*

Right and wrong kinds of Tolerance

Toleration without purity and candour is dangerous. . . . It is a perverse compassion which looks on without venturing to help a neighbour from out of the peril of sin by reaching forth a hand in the shape of a kind but honest remonstrance. . . . One should forbear in all things . . . short of offending God. This is the limit of all true forbearance [but] impetuous zeal without wisdom or moderation does more harm than good.

Jean Pierre Camus: *The Spirit of S. Francis de Sales* (trans. H. L. Sidney Lear)

Tolerance, far from being indifferent, depends on the fact of difference: it is a way of meeting difference which has been clearly recognised as such; and we cannot meet difference unless we are sufficiently interested in it to feel its challenge and to wrestle with it. . . . Before we ever become capable of tolerance, and before it can ever exist in any true sense, we must be shaken by the recognition that there are profound differences between ourselves and others, and that nobody can be really indifferent to the truths which imbue his whole existence. What we have to fear much more [than these differences] is that pseudo-tolerant attitude that takes neither one's own nor the other man's beliefs seriously enough to battle about them . . . tolerance can become the watchword of a philosophy of life which excludes all others under the pretext that they are narrow and intolerant. This, of course, is not tolerance but budding intolerance. . . Jaspers* makes the point that "indifference is born . . . of the arrogance of one's own truth and is the mildest form of intolerance: secret contempt—let others believe what they like, it doesn't concern me."

It is the duty of all intelligent people continually to question, not seldom to disbelieve, what they are told. . . .

Scepticism, however, is not a sufficient index, or the sole duty, of an intelligent person: it must be balanced by some genuine enthusiasm. Disbelief alone leads to sterility, it must be examined just as critically as belief, its emotional basis must be sought. Those who disbelieve from ignorance and meanness are as many as those who believe from stupidity or laziness. Faith is not necessarily a sign of mental infirmity. Most men are fundamentally good and kind, not a few, in some respects at least, are far-seeing and wise. The problems of life, of medicine, of politics, of international relations, of economics, lack simple solutions not merely because of the stupidity and baseness of mankind. It is safer to have faith without evidence than to doubt without cause.

Criticism is the basis of scientific advance, of social and ethical progress: it is also the cornerstone of intellectual honesty, of the conservatism which preserves as well as creates. To be uncritical, particularly of oneself and one's ideas and motives, is the first long step towards dishonesty. Much criticism, however, is mean, mean indeed in its ancient sense of wicked. It is mean to pretend that politics is necessarily a "dirty game": to imagine that piety is

* Karl Jaspers: *The Origin and Goal of History*

always a pretence. It is mean to sneer at those who carry a heavier burden than one's own. Let us laugh at, and—by good fortune—with, those from whom we differ: let us recognize, however, that they are probably neither criminal nor insane, that we also may be wrong.

A. V. Hill: *The Ethical Dilemma of Science*

The concept of an almost unlimited inner freedom, as it has been conveyed to the working classes through increasingly shallow channels, has flowed into and absorbed the older notion of tolerance, and taken it much farther than it had gone before. . . . I am thinking . . . of the manner in which the concept of freedom has been transmitted, of the muddled but nevertheless strong assumption that old sanctions have been finally removed, that "science" has altogether removed the claims of religion, that psychology has justified the utmost "broadmindedness".

The popularizers reinforce, with a flattering mushiness, the old phrase that "after all, it's only 'uman" with the suggestion that "scientists tell us" that "inhibitions are all wrong". It was always a comfort to think that nature free is also naturally good; now we know. This becomes very soon the idea of freedom as a justification. It is always freedom from, never freedom for. . . . Thus the concept of freedom may widen until it becomes the freedom not to "be" anything at all, and certainly hardly to object to anything at all. A man is free not to choose, but if he uses his freedom to choose so as to be unlike the majority, he is likely to be called "narrow-minded", "bigoted", "dogmatic", "intolerant" . . . "Anything goes" is related to "live and let live", but carries the matter a good deal farther; the open mind has become a yawning chasm. Tolerance becomes not so much a charitable allowance for human frailty and the difficulties of ordinary lives, as a weakness. . . . The tolerance of men who have some strength and are prepared, if necessary, to use it, is a meaningful tolerance; the tolerance of those whose muscles are flabby and spirits unwilling is simply a "don't-hit-me" masquerading as mature agreement. Genuine tolerance is a product of vigour, belief, a sense of the difficulty of truth, and a respect for others; the new tolerance is weak and unwilling, a fear and resentment of challenge.

Richard Hoggart: *The Uses of Literacy*

True tolerance is often painful—to allow ideas that seem to us pernicious to have their say and run their course; to watch the Adversary "going to and fro in the earth and walking up and down in it" unhindered. That is difficult and distressing. Indifference is false tolerance and it is easy. It is characteristic of an age which has neither a clear philosophy of life nor a strong framework of traditional morals; hence it is common to-day. But Plato was right to put lowest but one in the scale of human beings the type which he calls "the democratic man" whose "life is subject to no order or restraint".

Sir Richard Livingstone: *Tolerance in Theory and Practice*

SECOND PART

ACCEPTANCE

Tolerance involves Acceptance—in humility, of our own limitations, in charity, of the unlovely and sinful, and in patience and magnanimity, of other people's opinions and points of view.

The Acceptance of the tolerant is a creative attitude, as different as possible from resignation or condonation or indifference.

I

Acceptance of "the burden and the mystery", of our own limitations and of decay and death

Our Fallibility and the shortness of our Knowledge should make us peaceable and gentle: because I may be Mistaken, I *must* not be dogmatical and confident, peremptory and imperious. I will not break the certain laws of Charity for a doubtful Doctrine or uncertain Truth.

Benjamin Whichcote

Things are greater than we, and will not comply with us; we, who are less than things must comply with them.

Benjamin Whichcote

We should be low and loverlike, and loyal, each man to other,
And pacient as pilgrims, for pilgrims are we alle.

Langland

How did the great rivers and seas get their kingship over the hundred lesser streams? Through the merit of being lower than they: that was how they got their kingship.

What is of all things the most yielding, and can overwhelm that which is of all things most hard? The highest good is like that of water. The goodness of water is that it benefits the ten thousand creatures, yet itself it does not scramble but is content with the places that all men disdain. It is this that makes Water so near to the Way.

Lao Tze: *Tao tê Ching* (trans. Arthur Waley)

One of my greatest "openings" into the mystery of religion came from something I heard Oscar Wilde say in Philadelphia, dressed in shorts with a big sunflower in his buttonhole. He said, "You can conquer a city by force, but you can only conquer the Art of that city by submission to its rules".

Mrs. Pearsall Smith: *Letters*

As a rule we disbelieve all facts and theories for which we have no use . . . To know is one thing and to know for certain that we know is another. . . . But now, since we are all such absolutists by instinct, what in our quality of students of philosophy ought we to do about the fact? Shall we espouse and endorse it? or shall we treat it as a weakness of our nature from which we must free ourselves if we can? I sincerely believe that the latter course is the only one we can follow as reflective men. Objective evidence and certitude are doubtless very fine ideals to play with, but where on this moonlit and dream visited planet are they found?

. . . But please observe, now, that when as empiricists we give up the doctrine of objective certitude, we do not thereby give up the quest or hope of truth itself. We still pin our faith on its existence and still believe that we gain an even better position towards it by systematically continuing to roll up experiences and think.

William James: *The Will to Believe*

This gentleness and quietness of Reason doth never commend it self more, than in its agreeing and complying with Faith; in not opposing those high and transcendent Mysteries, that are above its own reach and capacity: nay it had always so much humility and modesty waiting and attending upon it, that it would always submit and subordinate it self to all such Divine Revelations, as were above its own Sphere. Though it could not grasp them, though it could not pierce into them; yet it ever resolv'd with all gratitude to admire them, to bow its head and to adore them. One Light does not oppose another.

Nathaniel Culverwel

Since it is impossible to deny secular alterations in our sentiments and needs, it would be absurd to affirm that one's own age of the world can be beyond correction by the next age. Skepticism cannot, therefore, be ruled out by any set of thinkers as a possibility against which their conclusions are secure; and no empiricist ought to claim exemption from this universal liability. But to admit one's liability to correction is one thing, and to embark upon a sea of wanton doubt is another. Of willfully playing into the hands of skepticism we cannot be accused. He who acknowledges the imperfectness of his instrument, and makes allowance for it in discussing his observations, is in a much better position for gaining truth than if he claimed his instrument to be infallible. Or is dogmatic or scholastic theology less doubted in point of fact for claiming, as it does, to be in point of right undoubtable? And if not, what command over truth would this kind of theology really lose if, instead of absolute certainty, she only claimed reasonable probability for her conclusions? If we claim only reasonable probability, it will be as much as men who love the truth can ever at any given moment hope to have within their grasp. Pretty surely it will be more than we could have had, if we were unconscious of our liability to err.

William James: *The Varieties of Religious Experience*

Humility before the Truth

We are not always bound to reject everything as false, that we know not how to reconcile with something that is true. . . . I have sometimes thought God and men enjoy truth as differingly as they do time. For we men enjoy time but by parcels and always leave far the greatest part of it unreached by us; so we know but some particular truths, and are ignorant of far more than we attain to. Whereas God, as His eternity reaches to all the portions of time, so His omniscience gives Him at one view a prospect of the whole extent of truth; upon which account He sees all particular truths, not only distinct, but in their system and sees a connexion between those, that to us seemed the most distant ones. . . .

We ought not always to condemn the opinion which is liable to ill consequences, and incumbered with great inconveniences. . . . We must not expect to be able . . . to resolve all difficulties, and answer all objections, since we can never directly answer those, which require for their solution a perfect comprehension of what is infinite.

Sir Robert Boyle

Mountains were formed as carelessly as I,
Volcanoes throw them and the lightning cleft,
And they are burnt and frozen casually.
So is their beauty past our understanding,
Only we clearly see as beautiful
Their change from glowing red at morning time

To violet shadows after evening rain.
Dazed by magnificence, we love alone
The ordered day with passion intimate.
Eagerly too we welcome on their height
The green new growth of the audacious pines,
Like us once frail, soon fair, and soon to die.
But, understanding these, we may not lack
Humility and great tranquillity
To watch for what transcends our ordered minds,
Grandeur chaotic and unknowable.

Ethel Street: *Poems*

There is no royal road in these matters. . . . The unchartered surrounds us on every side and we must needs have some relation towards it, a relation which will depend on the general discipline of a man's mind and the bias of his whole character. As far as knowledge and conscious reason will go, we should follow resolutely their austere guidance. When they cease, as cease they must, we must use as best we can those fainter powers of apprehension and surmise and sensitiveness by which, after all, most high truth has been reached as well as most high art and poetry: careful always really to seek for truth and not for our own emotional satisfaction, . . . and remembering above all to walk gently in a world where the lights are dim and the very stars wander.

Gilbert Murray: *Four Stages of Greek Religion*

The excellence of every art is its intensity, capable of making all disagreeables evaporate, from their being in close relationship with Beauty and Truth. Examine 'King Lear' and you will find this exemplified throughout.

. . . I had not a dispute but a disquisition with Dilke on various subjects; several things dovetailed in my mind, and at once it struck me what quality went to form a Man of Achievement, especially in Literature, and which Shakespeare possessed so enormously—I mean Negative Capability, that is, when a man is capable of being in uncertainties, mysteries, doubts, without any irritable reaching after fact and reason.

Keats: *Letters*

But, if thou canst take this light of reason that is in thee, this poor snuffe, that is almost out in thee, thy faint and dimme knowledge of God, that riseth out of this light of nature, if thou canst in those embers, those cold ashes, finde out one small coale, and wilt take the paines to kneell downe, and blow that coale with thy devout Prayers, and light thee a little candle, (a desire to reade that Booke, which they call the Scriptures, and the Gospell, and the Word of God); If with that little candle thou canst creep humbly into low and poore places, if thou canst finde thy Saviour in a Manger... thou shalt never envy the lustre and glory of the great lights of worldly men, which are great by the infirmity of others, or by their own opinion.

John Donne: *Sermons*

Acceptance of other's joy

The bliss of other men is my delight,
  (When once my principles are right):
And every soul which mine doth see
  A treasury.
The face of God is goodness unto all,
And while He thousands to His throne doth call,
  While millions bathe in pleasures,
  And do behold His treasures,
    The joys of all
    On mine do fall,
And even my infinity doth seem
A drop without them of a mean esteem.

Where goodness is within, the soul doth reign.
  Goodness the only Sovereign!
  Goodness delights alone to see
  Felicity.
And while the Image of His goodness lives
  In me, whatever He to *any* gives
  Is my delight and ends
  In me, in all my friends:
    For goodness is
    The spring of bliss,
And 'tis the end of all it gives away
And all it gives it ever doth enjoy.

Traherne

A Brother asked an old man, saying, "What is humility?" And the old man answered and said unto him, "That thou payest not back evil for evil". That brother said unto him, "And supposing that a man cannot attain to this measure, what must we do?" The old man said unto him, "Let us flee and follow after silence".

The Paradise of the Fathers

Judge not the preacher, for He is thy judge;
If thou mislike him, thou conceiv'st Him not:
God calleth preaching folly: do not grudge
To pick out treasures from an earthen pot:
The worst speak something good; if all want sense,
God takes a text, and preacheth patience.

George Herbert: *The Church Porch*

It is very important for us to realize that God does not lead us all by the same road. . . . Remember that there must be someone to cook the meals and count yourselves happy in being able to serve like Martha. Reflect that true humility consists to a great extent in being ready for what the Lord desires to do with you.

Remember that the Lord walks among the pots and pans and that He will help you in the inward tasks and in the outward too.

St. Teresa: *The Way of Perfection and the Foundations* (trans. E. A Peers)

Give me humility and peace,
Contented thoughts, innoxious ease.
A sweet, revengeless, quiet minde.
And to my greatest haters, kinde.
Give me, my God! a heart as milde
And plain, as when I was a childe.

Henry Vaughan

A portrait of love and humility in Age

[Rufinus of Aquileia in his preface to *The History of the Monks of Egypt* writes thus of the Desert Fathers:]

I have seen among them many fathers that lived the life of heaven in the world . . . I have seen some of them so purged of all thought or suspicion of malice that they no more remembered that evil was still wrought upon the earth . . . They dwell dispersed throughout the desert and separate in their cells, but bound together by love . . . Quiet are they and gentle . . . They have indeed a great rivalry among them . . . it is who shall be more merciful than his brother, kinder, humbler, more patient. If any be more learned than the rest, he carries himself so commonplace and ordinary towards all that he seems to be as Our Lord said the least among them and the servant of them all. . . . So because God gave me this boon, that I saw them and shared their life, I shall now try to tell of them, one by one, as God shall bring them to my mind: so that those who have not seen them in the body may by reading be drawn to imitate their holy toil, and seek the palm of perfect wisdom of patience.

A portrait of love and humility in Youth

I have never known Christopher to be downcast or angry for more than a few minutes at a stretch. He was lighthearted by nature and was generous in sharing his happiness. He was tolerant of men less gifted and less constant than himself. We had a good deal of hardship but he was never angered or depressed by it. He had a vast catholic zest for life. He could close his mind to stupidity, meanness, coarseness in men and love them for what was good in them. He could palliate the horrible cruelty of Indians to animals because they were loving to one another and to children. We used to discuss that. I hated Indians, I still hate them, for their cruelty to their horses and cattle and for their cold passivity to the sufferings of old infirm diseased persons, or persons broken by poverty unless they were children or family or friends. Christopher understood this, and sympathised. He had the light of a forerunner which is denied to me and to most of us. He might have been John preparing the way for the consummation of a high vision to man. To be a John there must be a great love and great understanding and endurance and energy and faith beyond question. It was something of this that made me humble sometimes in our talks. I could have pin-pricked his light and faith with logic, and the pinpricks to a lesser faith and light would have been fatal, but to him they would have been pinpricks, and I knew that he was right and I was wrong. He had no desire for notoriety. He could have had notoriety by withholding some vital thing in his work, so that the origins must be sought and the originator would have been known. Perhaps my affection and respect for him are based first on this willing abnegation. I shall miss him as long as I live. We need his intensity and clarity of feeling and thought, his tolerance and his energy. It was all, by whatever roundabout means, to have been for the good of man. He could not have prevented it being for good although he might have remained ignorant all his life of what had been his real contribution.

Frank Prewett: *A letter on a Young Scientist*

You know the Countess has the qualities of true divinity.
For instance: how apparently undemandingly
She moves among us; and yet
Lives make and unmake themselves in her neighbourhood
As nowhere else. There are many names I could name
Who would have been remarkably otherwise
Except for her divine non-interference.

Christopher Fry: *The Dark is Light Enough*

O Almighty God, give to Thy servant a meek and gentle spirit, that I may be slow to anger, and easy to mercy and forgiveness. Give me a wise and constant heart, that I may never be moved to an intemperate anger for any injury that is done or offered. Lord, let me ever be courteous, and easy to be entreated; let me never fall into a peevish or contentious spirit, but follow peace with all men; offering forgiveness, inviting them by Courtesies, ready to confess my own errors, apt to make amends, and desirous to be reconciled. Let no sickness or cross accident, no employment or weariness, make me angry or ungentle and discontented, or unthankful, or uneasy to them that minister to me; but in all things make me like unto the holy Jesus.

Jeremy Taylor: *Prayers*

. . . I quite understand how you are both suffering yourself and causing others to suffer. You must work bravely and persistently in bearing the burden if you would relieve your neighbours. Everything like a proud or disdainful manner, all that savours of ridicule or censoriousness, indicates a self-satisfied mind, unconscious of its own foibles, a prey to fastidiousness, and finding pleasure in the troubles of others. There is nothing more humbling than this sort of pride; so easily wounded, disdainful, contemptuous, haughty, jealous of its own rights, implacable towards others. It is a proof that one is very imperfect indeed when one is so impatient with the imperfections of others. . . . Pray, read, humble yourself by cultivating lowly things. Soften your heart by uniting it to the Child Jesus in His Patience and Humiliation. Seek strength in silence. . . .

Fénelon: *Letters to Women*

Acceptance between lovers

Let me not to the marriage of true minds
Admit impediments: love is not love
Which alters when it alteration finds,
Or bends with the remover to remove.
O, no! it is an ever-fixèd mark,
That looks on tempests and is never shaken;
It is the star to every wandering bark,
Whose worth's unknown, although his height be taken.
Love's not Time's fool, though rosy lips and cheeks
Within his bending sickle's compass come;
Love alters not with his brief hours and weeks,
But bears it out even to the edge of doom:
If this be error and upon me proved,
I never writ, nor no man ever loved.

Shakespeare: *Sonnets*

Man must be lenient with his soul in her weaknesses and imperfections and suffer her failings as he suffers those of others, but he must not become idle, and must encourage himself to better things.

St. Seraphim of Sarov

People who love themselves aright, even as they ought to love their neighbour, bear charitably, though without flattery, with self as with another. They know what needs correction at home as well as elsewhere; they strive heartily and vigorously to correct it, but they deal with self as they would deal with some one else they wished to bring to God. They set to work patiently, not exacting more than is practicable under present circumstances from themselves any more than from others, and not being disheartened because perfection is not attainable in a day.

Fénelon: *Letters to Women*

Let us put up with ourselves in charity and try to rule ourselves as we should like to rule others. That is to say, using towards ourselves much gentle and persuasive skill, which will turn us inside out as delicately as we turn a glove. Use all your intelligence and experience in managing your own life, employing the tenderness you would expect to find in a being of ideal kindness.

. . . While accepting provisionally [the] influence of the physical on the moral, we must nevertheless try to obviate it, for it is not an ideal state. In order to do this be a little more tolerant towards yourself: do not try to force yourself to constant good efforts, whether interior or exterior, when you feel that tired nature implores you, as a poor cab-horse might ask its driver, to leave it alone and have pity on its impotence. . . . On this point, as on all others, great breadth and wisdom . . . If you are troubled, discontented, dull, anxious or fearful, say to yourself, "No! That does not come from my spirit! It does not come from me! Come! my Soul! Be at peace! Be happy! Reassure yourself! Be kind to yourself! Do not seriously impute any of this to yourself." Know that you live with God, that you are on good terms with Him, or what is even better, that God is on good terms with you.

Abbé de Tourville: *Letters* (trans. Lucy Menzies)

Love bade me welcome; yet my soul drew back,
  Guilty of dust and sin,
But quick-eyed Love, observing me grow slack
  From my first entrance in,

Drew nearer to me, sweetly questioning
  If I lacked anything.

"A guest," I answered, "worthy to be here."
  Love said, "You shall be he."
"I, the unkind, ungrateful? Ah, my dear,
  I cannot look on Thee."
Love took my hand and smiling did reply,
  "Who made the eyes but I?"

"Truth, Lord; but I have marred them: let my shame
  Go where it doth deserve."
"And know you not," says Love, "Who bore the blame?"
  "My dear, then I will serve."
"You must sit down," says Love, "and taste my meat."
  So I did sit and eat.

George Herbert: *Love*

We can see how great an antagonism may naturally arise between the healthy-minded way of viewing life and the way that takes all experience of evil as something essential. To this latter way, the morbid-minded way, as we might call it, healthy-mindedness pure and simple seems unspeakably blind and shallow. To the healthy-minded way, on the other hand, the way of the sick soul seems unmanly and diseased. . . . If religious intolerance and hanging and burning could again become the order of the day, there is little doubt that, however it may have been in the past, the healthy-minded would at present show themselves the less indulgent party of the two.

In our own attitude, not yet abandoned, of impartial onlookers, what are we to say of this quarrel? It seems to me that we are bound to say that morbid-mindedness ranges over the wider scale of experience, and that its survey is the one that overlaps. The method of averting one's attention from evil, and living simply in the light of good, is splendid as long as it will work. It will work with many persons; it will work far more generally than most of us are ready to suppose; and within the sphere of its successful operation there is nothing to be said against it as a religious solution. But it breaks down impotently as soon as melancholy comes; and even though one be quite free from melancholy one's self, there is no doubt that healthy-mindedness is inadequate as a philosophical doctrine, because the evil facts which it refuses positively to account for are a genuine portion of reality; and they may after all be the best key to life's significance, and possibly the only openers of our eyes to the deepest levels of truth.

William James: *The Varieties of Religious Experience*

We can get in touch with another person only by an attitude of unprejudiced objectivity. This may sound like a scientific precept, and may be confused with a purely intellectual and detached attitude of mind. But what I mean to convey is something quite different. It is a human quality—a kind of deep respect for facts and events and for the person who suffers from them—a respect for the secret of such a human life. The truly religious person has this attitude. He knows that God has brought all sorts of strange and inconceivable things to pass, and seeks in the most curious ways to enter a man's heart. He therefore senses in everything the unseen presence of the divine will. This is what I mean by "unprejudiced objectivity". It is a moral achievement on the part of the doctor, who ought not to let himself be repelled by illness and corruption. We cannot change anything unless we accept it. Condemnation does not liberate, it oppresses. I am the oppressor of the person I condemn, not his friend and fellow-sufferer. I do not in the least mean to say that we must never pass judgment in the cases of persons whom we desire to help and improve. But if the doctor wishes to help a human being he must be able to accept him as he is. And he can do this in reality only when he has already seen and accepted himself as he is.

C. G. Jung: *Modern Man in Search of a Soul*

Out of evil, much good has come to me. By keeping quiet, repressing nothing, remaining attentive, and, hand in hand with that, by accepting reality—taking things as they are, and not as I wanted them to be—by doing all this, rare knowledge has come to me, and rare powers as well, such as I could never have imagined before. I always thought that, when we accept things, they overpower us in one way or another. Now this is not true at all, and it is only by accepting them that one can define an attitude toward them. So now I intend playing the game of life, being receptive to whatever comes to me, good and bad, sun and shadow that are for ever shifting, and, in this way, also accepting my own nature with its positive and negative sides. Thus everything becomes more alive to me. What a fool I was! How I tried to force everything to go according to my idea!

A Patient's Letter to Jung

[Oceanus speaks in the Council of the Titans.]

O ye, whom wrath consumes! Who, passion-stung,
Writhe at defeat, and nurse your agonies!
Shut up your senses, stifle up your ears,
My voice is not a belllows unto ire.
Yet, listen, ye who will, whilst I bring proof
How ye, perforce, must be content to stoop;
And in the proof much comfort will I give,
If ye will take that comfort in its truth.
We fall by course of Nature's law, not force
Of thunder, or of Jove. Great Saturn, thou
Hast sifted well the atom-universe,
But for this reason, that thou art the King
And only blind from sheer supremacy,
One avenue was shaded from thine eyes,
Through which I wander'd to eternal truth.
And first, as thou wast not the first of powers,
So art thou not the last; it cannot be . . .

Now comes the pain of truth, to whom 'tis pain;
O folly! for to bear all naked truths,
And to envisage circumstance, all calm
That is the top of sovereignty. Mark well!
As Heaven and Earth are fairer, fairer far
Than Chaos and blank Darkness, though once chief
... So on our heels a fresh perfection treads,
A power more strong in beauty, born of us
And fated to excel us ... nor are we
Thereby more conquer'd than by us the rule
Of shapeless Chaos. Say, doth the dull soil
Quarrel with the proud forests it hath fed,
And feedeth still, more comely than itself?
Can it deny the chiefdom of green groves?
Or shall the tree be envious of the dove
Because it cooeth, and hath snowy wings
To wander wherewithal and find its joys?
We are such forest-trees, and our fair boughs
Have bred forth, not pale solitary doves,
But eagles golden-feathered, who do tower
Above us in their beauty, and must reign
In right thereof.

Keats: *Hyperion*

[Socrates accepts his death sentence, having been condemned by the State of Athens for subverting the morals of the young. Crito is trying to persuade him to escape.]

SOCRATES Then consider the matter in this way. Imagine that I am about to play truant (you may call the proceeding by any name which you like), and the laws and the government come and interrogate me: "Tell us, Socrates," they say; "What are you about? are you not going by an act of yours to overturn us—the laws, and the whole state, as far as in you lies? Do you imagine that a state can subsist and not be overthrown, in which the decisions of law have no power, but are set aside and trampled upon by individuals?" [Shall I reply] "Yes; but the state has injured me and given an unjust sentence." Suppose I say that?

CRITO Very good, Socrates.

SOCRATES "And was that our agreement with you?" the law would answer; "or were you to abide by the sentence of the state? . . . Tell us—What complaint have you to make against us which justifies you in attempting to destroy us and the state? . . . For, having brought you into the world, and nurtured and educated you, and given you and every other citizen a share in every good which we had to give, we further proclaim to any Athenian by the liberty which we allow him, that if he does not like us when he has become of age and has seen the ways of the city . . . he may go where he pleases and take his goods with him. But he who has experience of the manner in which we order justice and administer the state, and still remains, has entered into an implied contract that he will do as we command him.

"You, Socrates, are breaking the covenants and agreements which you made with us at your leisure, not in any haste or under any compulsion or deception, but after you have had seventy years to think of them, during which time you were at liberty to leave the city . . . you might have gone either to Lacedæmon or Crete, both of which states are often praised by you for their good government, or to some other Hellenic or foreign state. Whereas you, above all other Athenians, seemed to be so fond of the state, or in other words, of us her laws . . . that you never stirred out of her; the halt, the blind, the maimed were not more stationary in her than you were. And now you run away and forsake your agreements . . .

"Listen, then, Socrates, to us who have brought you up. Think not of life and children first, and of justice afterwards, but of justice first. . . . For neither will you nor any that belong to you be happier or holier or juster in this life, or happier in another, if you do as Crito bids. Now you depart in innocence, a sufferer and not a doer of evil; a victim, not of laws but of men. But if you go forth, returning evil for evil, and injury for injury, breaking the covenants and agreements which you have made with us, and wronging those whom you ought least to wrong, that is to say, yourself, your friends, your country and us, we shall be angry with you while you live, and our brethren, the laws in the other world, will receive you as an enemy; for they will know that you have done your best to destroy us. Listen, then, to us and not to Crito."

This, dear Crito, is the voice which I seem to hear murmuring in my ears like the sound of a flute in the ears of the mystic; that voice, I say, is humming in my ears, and prevents me from hearing any other. And I know that anything more which you may say will be vain. Yet speak, if you have anything to say.

CRITO I have nothing to say, Socrates.

SOCRATES Leave me then, Crito, to fulfil the will of God, and to follow whither he leads.

Plato: *Crito* (trans. B. Jowett)

[Socrates speaks to his judges.]

Wherefore, O judges, be of good cheer about death, and know of a certainty, that no evil can happen to a good man, either in life or after death. He and his are not neglected by the gods; nor has my own approaching end happened by mere chance. But I see clearly that the time had arrived when it was better for me to die and be released from trouble; wherefore the oracle gave no sign. For which reason, also, I am not angry with my condemners, or with my accusers; they have done me no harm, although they did not mean to do me any good; and for this I may gently blame them. ... The hour of departure has arrived, and we go on our ways—I to die, and you to live. Which is better God only knows.

Plato: *Apology* (trans. B. Jowett)

The course of life is fixed, and nature admits of its being run but in one way, and only once; and to each part of our life there is something specially seasonable; so that the feebleness of children, as well as the high spirits of youth, the soberness of maturer years, and the ripe wisdom of old age—all have a certain natural advantage which should be secured in its proper season. . . .

A short term of life is long enough for living well and honourably. But if you go farther, you have no more right to grumble than farmers do because the charm of the spring season is past and the summer and autumn have come. . . .

Cicero on Old Age (trans. E. S. Shuckburgh)

[Men must endure
Their going hence, even as their coming hither:
Ripeness is all. *King Lear*]

Where are the songs of spring? Ay, where are they?
Think not of them, thou hast thy music too,—
White barred clouds bloom the soft-dying day,
And touch the stubble-plains with rosy hue;
Then in a wailful choir the small gnats mourn
Among the river-sallows, borne aloft
Or sinking as the light wind lives or dies;
And full grown lambs loud bleat from hilly bourn;
Hedge-crickets sing; and now with treble soft
The red-breast whistles from a garden-croft;
And gathering swallows twitter in the skies.

John Keats: *Ode to Autumn*

II

Acceptance of the Unlovely, sinners, clowns, rogues and vagabonds

What a vile antithesis is that between a man and his faults! If I love a man I do not love his faults, for they are abstractions, but I love the man *in* his faults.

Mark Rutherford

Give me man as he ought not to be.

Charles Lamb

Bear with evil and expect Good.

Outlandish Proverbs
Selected by *George Herbert* 1639

And here, in dust and dirt, O here,
The lillies of His love appear.

Henry Vaughan

I often wonder at the blindness of human beings towards each other. When we observe each other do we only see what is within ourselves? The limitation of our own natures perhaps limits our understanding of others. When we condemn and criticize other people, it may be that we are really criticizing ourselves. The sensitive inner eye that can see into the depths of our fellows and feel their tangles and complexities under layer upon layer of habit is, I suppose, rare; for it demands a self purified from envy and malice, and lit by the penetrating lamp of love and understanding, and a sincere whole-hearted compassion for tangled shot-silk human nature.

Lady Ottoline Morrell: *Memoirs*

S. Francis de Sales objected to pronouncing any one to be wicked on account of a single bad action. "Good habits are not destroyed by one act of a contrary nature," he would say; "nor is it fair to call a man intemperate because of one act of intemperance, or the like." He was wont to point out the difference between vice and sin—one being a habit, the other an act. As one swallow does not make summer, so neither does it necessarily follow from one act of sin that a man is vicious. Someone observed that neither ought we hastily to pronounce anyone to be living in grace and charity, however holy his outward actions might appear. To this Francis replied that if, as S. James tells us, faith is known by its works, far more true is it of charity, which is a more active virtue; its works prove its existence, as sparks show where there is fire; and although in case of mortal sin we are constrained to admit that the sinner has forfeited grace, how can we say but that God may have touched his heart within the next moment, and that an act of contrition may not already have brought him back to the narrow road? Ever be slow to think evil of others, but use all freedom on the other side, because charity hopeth all things, believeth all things, and rejoiceth not in iniquity but in the truth.

Jean Pierre Camus: *The Spirit of S. Francis de Sales* (trans. H. L. Sidney Lear)

In the whole process which from first to last activates and directs the elements of the universe, everything forms a single whole.... Little by little, stage by stage, everything is finally linked to the supreme centre in *quo omnia constant*. The streams which flow from this centre operate not only within the higher reaches of the world, where human activities take place in a distinctively supernatural and meritorious form. In order to save and establish these sublime forces, the power of the Word Incarnate penetrates matter itself; it goes down into the deepest depths of the lower forces ... by virtue of the Creation and still more of the Incarnation, nothing here below is profane for those who know how to see.

Not everything is immediately good to those who seek God, but everything is capable of becoming good.... There is a time for growth and a time for diminishment in the lives of each one of us. At one moment the dominant note is one of constructive human effort, and at another mystical annihilation.

Pierre Teilhard de Chardin: *Le Milieu Divin*

One foot in Eden still, I stand
And look across the other land.
The world's great day is growing late,
Yet strange these fields that we have planted
So long with crops of love and hate.
Time's handiworks by time are haunted,
And nothing now can separate
The corn and tares compactly grown,
The armorial weed in stillness bound
About the stalk; these are our own.

Evil and good stand thick around
In the fields of charity and sin
Where we shall lead our harvest in.

Yet still from Eden springs the root
As clean as on the starting day.
Time takes the foliage and the fruit
And burns the archetypal leaf
To shapes of terror and of grief
Scattered along the winter way.
But famished field and blackened tree
Bear flowers in Eden never known.
Blossoms of grief and charity
Bloom in these darkened fields alone.
What had Eden ever to say
Of hope and faith and pity and love
Until was buried all its day
And memory found its treasure trove?
Strange blessings never in Paradise
Fall from these beclouded skies.

Edwin Muir: *One Foot in Eden*

Socrates and Alcibiades

Socrates had just finished his noble disposition upon the ascent of love—from beautiful bodies to beautiful morals and from beautiful morals to beautiful science and from the sciences finally "to that Science which is nothing less than the Science of pure Beauty"—when suddenly there was a great noise of knocking at the porch as if of revellers, and the piping of a flute girl was heard. Soon after the drunken voice of Alcibiades sounded from without, shouting loudly for Agathon and insisting on being brought to him. The flute girl and some of his other followers supported him as he stood in the doorway, crowned with a thick crown of ivy and violets and with many ribands on his head. He cried out "Hail all of you! may one who has drunk deeply join your company or must I leave as soon as I have crowned Agathon, which is what I am here for? I could not come yesterday, so I am here today and I am going to take this crown from my head and crown that of the wisest and most beautiful of men. Are you going to laugh at me for being drunk? Well, laugh away!" Alcibiades, after a little more drunken talk, came in without seeing Socrates, who quietly and courteously made room for him between himself and Agathon. Agathon told the slaves to unsandal Alcibiades so that he could lie down with them and make a third. "Who is the third drunkard, then?" enquired Alcibiades, and turning, suddenly saw Socrates. Then follows a glorious interchange of laughter, talk and teasing between the drunken reveller and the divine Philosopher. Finally a whole army of roysterers burst in and the place was filled with clamour. At length some went home, some fell asleep, but Socrates continued to speak of tragedy and comedy until at daybreak he left them all and went his way. When he reached the Lyceum he bathed and spent the rest of the day as usual.

Compiled from Plato's *Symposium*

And the scribes and pharisees brought unto him a woman taken in adultery; and when they had set her in the midst, they said unto him; "Master, this woman was taken in adultery, in the very act. Now Moses in the law commanded us that such should be stoned: but what sayest thou?"

This they said, tempting him, that they might have to accuse him. But Jesus stooped down, and with his finger wrote on the ground, as though he heard them not. So when they continued asking him, he lifted up himself, and said unto them, "He that is without sin among you, let him first cast a stone at her". And again he stooped down, and wrote on the ground.

And they which heard it, being convicted by their own conscience went out one by one, beginning at the eldest, even unto the last: and Jesus was left alone, and the woman standing in the midst. When Jesus had lifted up himself and saw none but the woman, he said unto her, "Woman, where are those thine accusers? hath no man condemned thee?"

She said, "No man, Lord". And Jesus said unto her, "Neither do I condemn thee: go, and sin no more".

St. John

And then was Queen Guenever ware of Sir Launcelot as he walked in the cloister. And when she saw him she swooned thrice. . . When Sir Launcelot was brought to her she said, "Sir Launcelot, wit thou well I am set in such a plight to get my soul-heal; and yet I trust through God's grace that after my death to have a sight of the blessed face of Christ . . . for as sinful as ever I was are saints in heaven; . . . therefore, Sir Launcelot, go to thy realm; and there take a wife and live with her in joy and bliss, and I pray thee heartily, pray for me to our Lord that I may amend my misliving." . . . And they departed. But there was never so hard an hearted man but he would have wept to see the dolour that they made.

And after Queen Guenever's death Sir Launcelot sorrowed exceedingly and said, "My sorrow was not, nor is not, for any rejoicing of sin, but my sorrow may never have an end. For when I remember of her beauty, and of her noblesse, that was both with her king and with her, so when I saw his corpse and her corpse so lie together, truly mine heart would not serve to sustain my careful body. Also when I remember me how by my default, mine orgule and my pride, that they were both laid full low, that were peerless that ever was living of Christian people, wit you well," said Sir Launcelot, "this remembered, of their kindness and mine unkindness sank so to mine heart, that I might not sustain myself." . . . Then Sir Launcelot never after ate but little meat, ne drank till he was dead. . . . And so after midnight, against day, the Bishop [that] then was hermit, as he lay in his bed asleep, he fell upon a great laughter. And therewith all the fellowship awoke, and came to the Bishop, and asked him what he ailed. "Ah Jesu mercy," said the Bishop, "why did ye awake me? I was never in all my life so merry and so well at ease." "Wherefore?" said Sir Bors. "Truly," said the Bishop, "here was Sir Launcelot with me with mo angels than ever I saw men in one day. And I saw the angels heave up Sir Launcelot unto heaven, and the gates of heaven opened against him." . . . So when Sir Bors and his fellows came to [Sir Launcelot's] bed they found him stark dead and he lay as he had smiled and the sweetest savour about him that ever they felt.

Sir Thomas Malory: *Morte D'Arthur*

Whatever we may understand by the "sinners" with whom Jesus consorted, it is quite certain that the publicans were rightly regarded by the Jews as oppressors. References to "publicans and sinners" are frequently quoted as though the phrase was an equivalent for "down and outs", but the most important thing, surely, is the fact that Jesus, who loved the poor and hated oppression, did not find it inconsistent to consort with the oppressive publicani. It had excellent results. One gave up his objectionable work and became a disciple; at least one other ("Zaccaeus, which was the chief among the publicans, and he was rich") took some very practical steps by way of repentance. Since, as Jesus said, publicans were among those who had accepted the teachings of John the Baptist (who had made what must have been a hard demand on them) there was probably a considerable change in the attitude of many tax-gatherers at that time. Again, we emphasize the fact that Jesus ate and drank with the publicans, but it is quite as important that the publicans should have accepted and even sought his company, as frequent references show. It cannot have been because they found any approval or sanction for extortion in the words of Christ. Quite on the contrary, he regarded them as sick men, having need of a physician, and classified them with harlots—very rightly, as they had prostituted their services, doing the least pleasant work of the Roman conquerors for the sake of money. They were "Quislings" and collaborators. But even this reference to "publicans and harlots" was not a condemnation of the men themselves, since Jesus made the harlots equally welcome.

Reginald Reynolds: *The Wisdom of John Woolman*

And treweliche, as writen wel I finde,
That al this thing was seyd of good entente;
And that his herte trewe was and kinde
Towards him, and spak right as she mente,
And that she starf for wo neigh, whan she wente,
And was in purpose ever to be trewe;
Thus writen they that of his werkes knewe.

I find eek in the stories elles-where,
Whan through the body hurt was Diomede
Of Troilus, tho weep she many a tere,
Whan that she saugh his wyde woundes blede;
And that she took to kepen him good hede,
And for to hele him of his sorwes smerte
Man seyn, *I not*, that she yat him hir herte.

But trewely, the story telleth us,
Ther made niver womman more wo
Than she, whan that she falsed Troilus,
She seyde, "allas! for now is clere a-go
My name of trouthe in love, for ever-mo.
For I have falsed oon, the gentileste
That ever was, and oon the worthieste."

But trewely, how longe it was bitwene,
That she for-sook him for this Diomede,
There is non auctor telleth it, I wene,
Take every man now to his bokes hede;
He shall no terme finden, out of drede.
For though that he bigan to wowe hir sone,
Er he hir wan, yet was ther more to done.

Ne me no list this sely womman chyde
Ferther than the story wol devyse,
Hir name, allas! is publisshed so wyde,
That for hir gilt it oughte y-now suffyse,
And if I mighte excuse hir any wyse,

For she so sorry was for hir untrouthe,
Y-wis, I wolde excuse hir yet for routhe.

Chaucer: *Troilus and Cressida*

From somewhere behind Curdie, crept forward the same hideous animal which had fawned at his feet at the door . . .

"Give Curdie a paw, Lina," said the princess.

The creature rose, and lifting a long fore leg, held up a great dog-like paw to Curdie. He took it gently. But what a shudder, as of terrified delight, ran through him when, instead of the paw of a dog, such as it seemed to his eyes, he clasped in his great mining fist the soft neat little hand of a child! . . . The green eyes stared at him with their yellow light, and the mouth was turned up towards him with its constant half-grin; but here *was* the child's hand! If he could but pull the child out of the beast? His eyes sought the princess. She was watching him with evident satisfaction.

"Ma'am, here is a child's hand!" said Curdie.

"Your gift does more for you than it promised. It is yet better to perceive a hidden good than a hidden evil."

George Macdonald: *The Princess and Curdie*

[This is a case of double tolerance—the tolerance of Heaven towards the soldier and the tolerance of the soldier towards Joan.]

(*A rough male voice is heard trolling an improvised tune*)

Rum tum trumpledum,
Bacon fat and rumpledum,
Old Saint mumpledum,
Pull his tail and stumpledum.
O my Ma—ry Ann!

(*A ruffianly English soldier comes through the curtains and marches between Dunois and Joan*)

DUNOIS What villianous troubadour taught you that doggrel?

SOLDIER No troubadour. We made it up ourselves as we marched. We were not gentlefolks and troubadours. Music straight out of the heart of the people, as you might say. Rum tum trumpledum, Bacon fat and rumpledum, Old Saint mumpledum, Pull his tail and stumpledum; that don't mean anything, you know; but it keeps you marching. Your servant, ladies and gentlemen. Who asked for a saint?

JOAN Be you a saint?

SOLDIER Yes, Lady, straight from hell.

DUNOIS A saint, and from hell!

SOLDIER Yes, noble captain: I have a day off. Every year, you know. That's my allowance for my one good action.

CAUCHON Wretch! In all the years of your life did you do only one good action?

SOLDIER I never thought about it: it came natural like. But they scored it up for me.

CHARLES What was it?

SOLDIER Why, the silliest thing you ever heard of. I—

JOAN (interrupting) He tied two sticks together, and gave them to a poor lass that was going to be burned.

SOLDIER Right. Who told you that?

JOAN Never mind. Would you know her if you saw her again?

SOLDIER Not I. There are so many girls! and they all expect you to remember them as if there was only one in the world. This one must have been a prime sort; for I have a day off every year for her; and so, until twelve o'clock punctually, I am a saint, at your service, noble lords and lovely ladies.

CHARLES And after twelve?

SOLDIER After twelve, back to the only place fit for the likes of me.

JOAN Back there! You! that gave the lass the cross!

SOLDIER (excusing his unsoldierly conduct) Well, she asked for it; and they were going to burn her. She had as good a right to a cross as they had; and they had dozens of them. It was her funeral, not theirs. Where was the harm in it?

G. B. Shaw: *St. Joan*

[Dr. Johnson wrote a life of Savage—a minor eighteenth-century poet whose reputation for dissolute living and violent temper could hardly have been worse. Johnson does not ignore or cover up his defects but concludes thus:]

For his life, or for his writings, none, who candidly consider his fortune, will think an apology either necessary or difficult. If he was not always sufficiently instructed in his subject, his knowledge was at least greater than could have been attained by others in the same state. If his works were sometimes unfinished, accuracy cannot reasonably be exacted from a man oppressed with want, which he had no hope of relieving but by a speedy publication. The indolence and resentment of which he is accused were not easily to be avoided by a great mind, irritated by perpetual hardships, and constrained hourly to return the spurns of contempt, and repress the indolence of prosperity; and vanity may surely readily be pardoned in him, to whom life afforded no other comforts than barren praises, and the consciousness of deserving them.

Those are no proper judges of his conduct, who have slumbered away their time on the down of plenty; nor will any wise man presume to say, "Had I been in Savage's condition, I should have lived or written better than Savage."

[On the quarrel between Savage and Steele. Steele had befriended Savage and had afterwards discovered that Savage had ridiculed him. Johnson comments:]

It is not indeed unlikely that Savage might by his imprudence expose himself to the malice of a tale-bearer. . . . A little knowledge of the world is sufficient to discover that such weakness is very common, and that there are few who do not sometimes, in the wantonness of thoughtless mirth or the heat of transient resentment, speak of their friends and benefactors with levity and contempt, though in their cooler moments they want neither sense of their kindness nor reverence for their virtue. The fault therefore of Mr. Savage was rather negligence than ingratitude; but Sir Richard must likewise be acquitted of severity; for who is there that can patiently bear contempt from one he has relieved and supported?

Dr. Johnson: *Lives of the Poets*

[The building of the choir of Canterbury Cathedral has been entrusted to William of Sens, whose character is denounced by the monk Theodatus.]

THEODATUS Skill is not all.
The Kingdom of Heaven is won by righteousness,
Not skill, He cannot wish His work performed
Save with clean hands and a pure heart.

PRIOR My son,
Will you not let God manage His own business?
He was a carpenter, and knows His trade
Better, perhaps, than we do, having had
Some centuries of experience; nor will He,
Like a bad workman, blame the tools wherewith
He builds His City of Zion here on earth.
For God founded His Church, not upon John,
The loved disciple, that lay so close to His heart
And knew His mind—not upon John, but Peter;
Peter the liar, Peter the coward, Peter
The rock, the common man. John was all gold,
And gold is rare; the work might wait while God
Ransacked the corners of the earth to find
Another John; but Peter is the stone
Whereof the world is made.

Dorothy L. Sayers: *The Zeal of Thy House*

Why have we indignation with the multitude? "They are robbers," one saith, and thieves. And what is it to be robbers and thieves? It is to err concerning things good and evil. Shall we, then, have indignation with them, or shall we pity them?

Should not, then, this robber, or this adulterer, be destroyed? By no means, but take it rather this way: This man who errs concerning things of greatest moment . . . should we not destroy him? And thus speaking, you shall know how inhuman is that which you say, and how like as if you said, "Shall we not destroy this blind man, this deaf man?" For if it is the greatest injury to be deprived of the greatest things, and the greatest thing in every man is a Will such as he ought to have, and one be deprived of this, why are you still indignant with him? . . . Pity him rather, be not inclined to offence and hatred. How have you suddenly become so wise and hard to please? Wherefore, then, have we indignation? Because we worship the things which they deprive us of and as long as thou dost value these things be angry with thyself rather than with others.

Arrian: *The Encheiridion of Epictetus* (trans. T. W. Rollerton)

[Robert Browning in the old Morgue.]

First came the silent gazers; next
A screen of glass, we're thankful for;
Last, the sight's self, the sermon's text,
The three men who did most abhor
Their life in Paris yesterday,
So killed themselves; and now enthroned
Each on his copper couch, they lay
Fronting me, waiting to be owned.
I thought, and think, then sin's atoned.

Poor men, God made, and all for that!
The reverance struck me; o'er each head
Religiously was hung his hat,
Each coat dripped by the owner's bed

Sacred from touch: each had his berth
His bounds, his proper place of rest,
Who last night tenanted on earth
Some arch, where twelve such slept abreast—
Unless the plain asphalte seemed best.

*

It's wiser being good than bad;
It's safer being meek than fierce:
It's fitter being sane than mad.
My own hope is, a sun will pierce
The thickest cloud earth ever stretched;
That, after Last, returns the First,
Though a wide compass round be fetched;
That what began best, can't end worst,
Nor what God blessed once, prove accurst.

Browning: *Apparent Failure*

Insolence and ingratitude made no difference to Diderot. His ear always remained open to every tale of distress, his sensibility always as quickly touched, his time, money and service always as profusely bestowed. I know not whether to say that this was made more, or that it was made less, of a virtue by his excess of tolerance for social castaways and reprobates. Our rough mode of branding a man as bad revolted him. The common appetite for constituting ourselves public prosecutors for the universe was to him one of the worst of human weaknesses. "You know," he used to say, "all the impetuosity of the passions; you have weighed all circumstances in your everlasting balance; you pass sentence on the goodness or the badness of creatures; you set up rewards and penalties among matters which have no proportion nor relation with one another. Are you sure that you have never committed wrong acts for which you pardoned yourselves, because their object was so slight, though at bottom they implied more wickedness than a crime prompted by misery or fury? Even magistrates supported by experience, by the law, by conventions which force them sometimes to give judgment against the testimony of their own conscience, still tremble as they pronounce the doom of the accused. And since when has it been lawful for the same person to be at once judge and informer?" Such reasoned leniency is the noblest of traits in a man. "I am more affected," he said, in words of which better men than Diderot might often be reminded, "by the charms of virtue than by the deformity of vice; I turn mildly away from the bad, and I fly to embrace the good. If there is in a work, in a character, in a painting, in a statue, a single fine bit, then on that my eyes fasten; I see only that, that is all I remember; the rest is as good as forgotten."

This is the secret of a rare and admirable temperament.

John Morley: *Diderot*

The ruined spendthrift, now no longer proud,
Claimed kindred there, and had his claims allow'd;

The broken soldier, kindly bade to stay,
Sat by his fire, and talked the night away;
Wept o'er his wounds, or tales of sorrow done,
Shoulder'd his crutch, and showed how fields were won.

Pleased with his guests, the good man learned to glow,
And quite forgot their vices in their woe;
Careless their merits or their faults to scan,
His pity gave e're charity began.

Oliver Goldsmith: *The Deserted Village*

[Erasmus and Sir Thomas More have made a pilgrimage to Canterbury together. On the way back the following incident occurs.]

In our journey to London, not far from Canterbury, there's a narrow, hollow, steep Way, and a cragged steep Bank on either Side, so that you can't escape it; for there is no other Way to go. Upon the left Hand of that Way, there is a little Cottage of old Mendicants. As soon as they espy a Man on Horseback coming, one of them runs out, and sprinkles him with holy Water, and then offers him the upper Leather of a Shoe . . . Having kiss'd it, you give a small Piece of Money . . . Gratian (Sir Thomas More) rode on my left Hand, next to this Cottage; he was sprinkled with holy Water, and took it pretty well; but upon presenting the Shoe, he ask'd what was meant by that? This, says the poor Man, was St. Thomas's Shoe. Gratian fell into a Passion, and turning to me, said, What would these Brutes have? Will they make us kiss the Shoes of all that have been good Men? Why do they not as well give us their Spittle, and other Excrements of their Bodies, to kiss? I pitied the poor old Man, and Comforted him, being sorrowful, by giving him a little Money. . . . In those Matters that cannot be mended on a sudden, it is my Way to make the best of them.

Colloquies of Erasmus. The Religious Pilgrimage

The professing satirist says that his target is hypocrisy . . . [and] since the particular incongruity which he professes to aim at is morally ugly, the ugliest of the possible incongruities between being and seeming, he cannot condone it. How could he exclaim with Elizabeth Bennet, "Follies and nonsense, whims and inconsistencies do divert me, I own, and I laugh at them whenever I can"—thankful, indeed, that the provision of them is never likely to fail—when the beast that he says he is hunting is one which he must wish to destroy? . . . But to Jane Austen, so far as they are not seriously harmful, they are altogether pleasant, because they are both ridiculous and right. . . . [there is] an affinity between her fools and Shakespeare's . . . When Sir Andrew Aguecheek ends his challenge "God have mercy on one of our souls! He may have mercy on mine, but my hope is better"—something strange is happening. What is opaque in life has become translucent in art. . . . But when daylight shines through Sir Andrew it is not because we are different from him, superior to him that we can see it, but because we are akin—because his simplicity . . . is nothing but a drop of human simplicity, and therefore of our simplicity.

. . . How does this capacity for sympathy with folly square with Jane Austen's moral purpose? It squares very well. She has among her characters some (such as Mrs. Elton) in whom what is ridiculous is quarry for the satirist. . . . But—and this is what matters—they are not distinguished by their folly; there is not a line drawn across, with the odious and foolish on one side of it and the amiable and wise on the other. . . . Along such a line Miss Bates—with the endearing absurdity of her comment on Mrs. Elton's arrival: "It is such a happiness when good people get together—and they always do"—would be forever straying.

Mary Lascelles: *Jane Austen and her Art*

FALSTAFF There is Percy: if your father will do me any honour, so; if not, let him kill the next Percy himself. I look to be either earl or duke, I can assure you.

PRINCE Why, Percy I killed myself, and saw thee dead.

FALSTAFF Didst thou? Lord, lord! how this world is given to lying. I grant you I was down and out of breath, and so was he; but we rose both at an instant, and fought a long hour by Shrewsbury clock. If I may be believed, so; if not, let them that should reward valour bear the sin upon their own heads. I'll take it upon my death, I gave him this wound in the thigh: if the man were alive and would deny it, 'zounds, I would make him eat a piece of my sword.

LANCASTER This is the strangest tale that e'er I heard.

PRINCE This is the strangest fellow, brother John.
Come, bring your luggage nobly on your back:
For my part, if a lie may do thee grace,
I'll gild it with the happiest terms I have.

Shakespeare: *Henry IV, Part I*

What is there wrong, pray, or shocking in the clown acting the clown? See that the fault does not lie rather at your own door, for not expecting him to go wrong thus. . . . When you complain of some breach of faith or gratitude, take heed first and foremost to yourself. Obviously the fault lies with yourself, if you had faith that a man of that disposition would keep faith, or if in doing a kindness you did not do it upon principle, nor upon the assumption that the kind act was to be its own reward. What more do you want in return for a service done? . . . Man is made for kindness, and whenever he does an act of kindness or otherwise helps forward the common good, he thereby fulfils the law of his being and comes by his own.

Marcus Aurelius

PHILOSTRATE

A play there is, my Lord, some ten words long,
Which is as brief as I have known a play:
But by ten words, my Lord, it is too long,
Which makes it tedious. . . .

THESEUS

What are they that do play it?

PHILOSTRATE

Hard-handed men, that work in Athens here,
Which never labour'd in their minds till now,
And now have toil'd their unbreath'd memories
With this same play, against your nuptial.

THESEUS

And we will hear it.

PHILOSTRATE

No, my noble Lord;
It is not for you: I have heard it over,
And it is nothing, nothing in the world:
Unless you can find sport in their intents . . .

THESEUS

I will hear that play:
For never anything can be amiss
When simpleness and duty tender it.
Go, bring them in. . . .

Hippolyta
I love not to see wretchedness o'er charg'd
And duty in his service perishing.

Theseus
Why, gentle sweet, you shall see no such thing.

Hippolyta
He says they can do nothing in this kind.

Theseus
The kinder we, to give them thanks for nothing.
Our sport shall be to take what they mistake:
And what poor duty cannot do, noble respect
Takes it in might not merit.
Where I have come, great clerks have purposed
To greet me with premeditated welcomes;
Where I have seen them shiver and look pale,
Make periods in the midst of sentences,
Throttle their practis'd accent in their fears,
And, in conclusion, dumbly have broke off,
Not paying me a welcome. Trust me, sweet,
Out of this silence, yet I pick'd a welcome;
And in the modesty of fearful duty
I read as much as from the rattling tongue
Of saucy and audacious eloquence.
Love, therefore, and tongue-tied simplicity
In least, speak most, to my capacity.

Shakespeare: *Midsummer Night's Dream*

[Dr. Johnson harboured "whole nests of people in his house", and when asked once why he gave money so often to beggars answered, "Madam, to enable them to beg on." The following anecdote is from the memoirs of Miss Burvey.]

"I have known all the wits; from Mrs. Montague down to Bet Flint!"

"Bet Flint!" cried Mrs. Thrale, "pray who is she?"

"Oh, a fine character, madam! She was habitually a slut and a drunkard, and occasionally a thief and a harlot."

"And for heaven's sake, how came you to know her?"

"Why madam, she wrote her own life . . . and brought me her verses to correct; but I gave her half-a-crown, and she liked it as well. Bet had a fine spirit; . . . oh I loved Bet Flint." . . .

"Bless me sir!" cried Mrs. Thrale, "how can all these vagabonds contrive to get at *you*, of all people?"

"O the dear creatures!" cried he, laughing heartily. "I can't but be glad to see them!"

The Festival of the Birth of Krishna

Down in the sacred corridors, joy had seethed to jollity. It was their duty to play various games to amuse the newly born God, and to simulate his sports with the wanton dairymaids of Brindaban. Butter played a prominent part in these. When the cradle had been removed, the principal nobles of the state gathered together for an innocent frolic. They removed their turbans, and one put a lump of butter on his forehead, and waited for it to slide down his nose into his mouth. Before it could arrive, another stole up behind him, snatched the melting morsel, and swallowed it himself. All laughed exultantly at discovering that the divine sense of humour coincided with their own. . . . There is fun in heaven. God can play practical jokes upon Himself, draw chairs away from beneath His own posterior, set His own turbans on fire, and steal His own petticoats when He bathes. By sacrificing good taste, this worship achieved what Christianity has shirked: the inclusion of merriment. All spirit as well as all matter must participate in salvation, and if practical jokes are banned the circle is incomplete.

E. M. Forster: *A Passage to India*

After the meeting was over I went to John Audland's and there came John Story to me and lighted his pipe of tobacco. And said he,

"Will you take a pipe of tobacco?", saying, "Come, all is ours." And I looked upon him to be a forward bold lad; and the tobacco I did not take, but it came into my mind that the lad might think that I had not unity with the creation. For I saw he had a flashy, empty notion of religion. So I took his pipe and put it to my mouth.

George Fox: *Journal*

I once complained of certain petty gentlefolk in the neighbourhood who, although they were as poor as Job, were likewise full of pretension, and for ever boasting of their high birth and the deeds of their ancestors. Francis turned round upon me in his graceful way, saying, "Would you strip these poor people of everything? If they are rich in dignities, it will help them to forget their actual poverty."

Jean Pierre Camus: *The Spirit of S. Francis de Sales* (trans. H. L. Sidney Lear)

III

Acceptance of Other People's Points of View

The right attitude towards your opponent
What to avoid and what to strive after in controversy

Those that differ upon Reason, may come together by Reason.
Benjamin Whichcote

To be prejudiced is always to be weak.
Dr. Johnson

The man who never alters his opinion is like standing water and breeds reptiles of the mind.
William Blake

An ancient prayer for tolerance

May I be no man's enemy, and may I be the friend of that which is eternal and abides. May I never quarrel with those nearest to me; and if I do, may I be reconciled quickly. May I never devise evil against any man; if any devise evil against me, may I escape uninjured and without the need of hurting him. May I love, seek, and attain only that which is good. May I wish for all men's happiness and envy none. May I never rejoice in the ill-fortune of one who has wronged me. . . . When I have done or said what is wrong, may I never wait for the rebuke of others, but always rebuke myself until I make amends. . . . May I win no victory that harms either me or my opponent. . . . May I reconcile friends who are wroth with one another. May I, to the extent of my power, give all needful help to my friends and to all who are in want. May I never fail a friend in danger. When visiting those in grief may I be able by gentle and healing words to soften their pain. . . . May I respect myself. . . . May I always keep tame that which rages within me. . . . May I accustom myself to be gentle and never be angry with people because of circumstances. May I never discuss who is wicked and what wicked things he has done, but know good men and follow in their footsteps.

Prayer of Eusobius (trans. Gilbert Murray)

Portrait of Benjamin Whichcote

He was slow to declare his judgement, and modest in delivering it. Never passionate, never peremptory; so far from imposing upon others that he was rather apt to yield. And though he had a most profound and well poised judgement, yet was he of all men I know the most patient to hear others differ from him, and the most easy to be convinced when good reason was offered; and, which is seldom seen, more apt to be favourable to another man's reason than his own. Studious and inquisitive men commonly at such an age (forty or fifty at the utmost) have fixed and settled their judgements in most points, and as it were made their last understanding, supposing they have thought, or read or heard what can be said on all sides of things; and after that, they grow positive and impatient of contradiction, thinking it a disparagement to them to alter their judgement. But our deceased friend was so wise as to be willing to learn to the last; knowing that no man can grow wiser without some change of mind, without gaining some knowledge which he had not, or correcting some error which he had before. He very seldom reproved any person in company otherwise than by silence, or some sign of uneasiness, or some very soft and gentle word; which yet from the respect men generally bore him did often prove effectual; for he understood human nature very well, and how to apply himself to it in the most easy and effectual ways.

Bishop Tillotson: *Funeral sermon on Benjamin Whichcote (one of the Cambridge Platonists)*

Had he had more of the wisdom of the serpent . . . he would perhaps have known that to try too hard to make people good is one way to make them worse; that the only way to make them good is to be good—remembering well the beam and the mote; that the time for speaking comes rarely, the time for being never departs.

George Macdonald: *Sir Gibbie*

A heated imagination, vehement feeling, a world of argument, and flow of words, are really useless. The practical thing is to act in a spirit of detachment, doing what one can by God's Light, and being content with such success as He gives. . . . When people let loose their natural excitability, they talk interminably, indulge endless, subtle, superfluous imaginations; they are afraid of not saying and doing enough,—they get warm, excited,—they exhaust themselves without anything being the better for it . . . Let everybody follow their natural disposition and habits; you cannot remould them, it is easier to let them alone and bear with them. Accustom yourself to put up with unreasonableness and injustice. Abide tranquilly in God's Bosom; He sees all these evils more clearly than you do, yet He suffers them. Be content with doing what little depends upon you well, and let all else be as though it were not.

Fénelon: *Letters to Women*

The true secret of giving advice is, after you have honestly given it, to be perfectly indifferent whether it is taken or not, and never persist in trying to set people right. That has been my secret, and I have never had any quarrels.

What if people are fools or knaves, it is not your housekeeping and you had far better leave them to their fate. The more you try to prove yourselves in the right and D. in the wrong, the more you will confirm him in his own views. Nothing makes people more furious than being proved to be in the wrong; and even if you convince D. he will always hate you.

Mrs. Pearsall Smith: *Letters*

I could never divide myself from any man upon the difference of an opinion, or be angry with his judgment for not agreeing with me in that, from which within a few days I should dissent myself. I have no genius to disputes in religion, and have often thought it wisdom to decline them, especially upon a disadvantage, or when the cause of truth might suffer in the weakness of my patronage. . . . Every man is not a proper champion for truth, nor fit to take up the gauntlet in the cause of verity. Many from the ignorance of these maxims, and an inconsiderate zeal unto truth, have too rashly charged the troops of error, and remain as trophies unto the enemies of truth. A man may be in as just possession of truth as of a city, and yet be forced to surrender; it is therefore far better to enjoy her with peace, than to hazard her on a battle: if therefore there rise any doubts in my way, I do forget them, or at least defer them till my better settled judgment and more manly reason be able to resolve them, for I perceive every man's own reason is his best Œdipus.

Sir Thomas Browne: *Religio Medici*

When I am impugned or contraried, then is mine attention and not mine anger stirred up: I advance my selfe toward him, that doth gainesay and instruct me. *The cause of truth ought to be the common cause, both to one and other*; What can he answer? The passion of choller hath already wounded his judgement: trouble, before reason hath seized upon it. It were both profitable and necessary, that the determining of our disputations might be decided by way of wagers; and that there were a materiall marke of our losses: that we might better remember and make more accompt of it: and that my boy might say unto me: Sir, if you call to minde; your contestation, your ignorance and your selfe-wilfulnesse, at severall times, cost you a hundred crownes the last yeare: I feast, I cherish and I embrace truth, where and in whom soever I finde it, and willingly and merily yeeld my selfe unto her, as soone as I see but her approach, though it be a farre-off, I lay downe my weapon and yeeld myself vanquished. And alwayes provided, one persist not or proceede therein, with an over imperious stiffnesse or commanding surlinesse; I am well pleased to be reprooved. And I often accommodate my selfe unto my accusers more by reason of civility, then by occasion of amendment: loving by the facility of yeelding, to gratifie and foster their libertie, to teach or advertise me. It is notwithstanding no easie matter to draw men of my times unto it. They have not the courage to correct, because they want the heart to endure correction: And ever speake with dissimulation in presence one of another. I take so great a pleasure to be judged and knowne, that it is indifferent to me, in whether of the two formes I be so. Mine owne imagination doth so often contradict and condemne it selfe, that if another do it, all is one unto me; especially seeing, I give his reprehension no other authority then I list. But I shall breake a straw or fall at ods with him, that keepes himselfe so aloft; as I know some, that will fret and chafe if their opinions be not believed, and who take it as an injury, yea and fall out with their best friends, if they will not follow it.

Montaigne: *Essays*. Third Book, Chapter VIII (trans. Florio)

[Asoka, ruler of India in 273 BC, writes in two edicts.]

The King honours all sects and both ascetics and laymen, with gifts and various forms of recognition. But the King does not consider gifts or honour to be as important as the advancement of the essential doctrine of all sects. This progress of the essential doctrine takes many forms, but its basis is the control of one's speech, so as not to extol one's own sect or disparage another's on unsuitable occasions, or at least to do so only mildly on certain occasions.

You should strive to practise impartiality. But it cannot be practised by one possessing any of these faults—jealousy, shortness of temper, harshness, rashness, obstinacy, idleness . . . The root of all this is to be even tempered and not rash.

Dr. F. W. Thomas: *Asoka* (*Cambridge History of India*)

The happiness of mankind is the end of virtue, and truth is the knowledge of the means; which he will never seriously attempt to discover, who has not habitually interested himself in the welfare of others. The searcher after truth must love and be beloved; for general benevolence is a necessary motive to constancy of pursuit; and this general benevolence is begotten and rendered permanent by social and domestic affections. . . . The man who would find truth must likewise seek it with an humble and simple heart.

Of this we may be certain, whether we be Christians or infidels, aristocrats or republicans, that our minds are in a state unsusceptible of knowledge, when we feel an eagerness to detect the falsehood of an adversary's reasonings, not a sincere wish to discover if there be truth in them;—when we examine an argument in order that we may answer it, instead of answering because we have examined it.

S. T. Coleridge: *From an Address delivered at Bristol in 1795*

A description of Charles Lamb

No politician ever laboured more to preserve the Balance of Power in Europe, than he did to correct any temporary preponderances. He was always trimming in the nautical, not the political sense. Thus in his "magnanimous letter", as Hazlitt called it, to High Church Southey, he professed himself a Unitarian. With a Catholic, he would probably have called himself a Jew: as among Quakers, by way of a set off against their own formality, he would indulge in a little extra levity. . . . If he was intolerant of anything, it was of intolerance.

Thomas Hood

There are, then, very many truths both in faith and morals which seem opposed, but which hold together in an astonishing order. All heresies spring from the exclusion of some of these truths. The reason of our objection to any heresy is its ignoring of some of our truths. Men are unable to imagine any relation between two opposing truths and so they assume that to state one is to deny the other.

Pascal: *Pensées*

[Socrates is discussing truth in argument with his friends on the last day of his life. The subject of the whole Dialogue is the immortality of the soul.]

SOCRATES . . . But first let us take care that we avoid a danger.

Of what nature? I said.

Lest we become misologists, he replied: no worse thing can

happen to a man than this. For as there are misanthropists or haters of men, there are also misologists or haters of ideas, and both spring from the same cause, which is ignorance of the world. . . . When a simple man who has no skill in dialectics believes an argument to be true which he afterwards imagines to be false, whether really false or not, and then another and another, he has no longer any faith left . . . and how melancholy, if there be such a thing as truth or certainty or possibility of knowledge—that a man should have lighted upon some argument or other which at first seemed true and then turned out to be false, and instead of blaming himself and his own want of wit, because he is annoyed, should at last be too glad to transfer the blame from himself to arguments in general: and for ever afterwards should hate and revile them, and lose truth and the knowledge of realities.

Yes, indeed, I said; that is very melancholy.

Let us then, in the first place, he said, be careful of allowing or of admitting into our souls the notion that there is no health or soundness in any arguments at all. Rather say that we have not yet attained to soundness in ourselves, and that we must struggle manfully and do our best to gain health of mind—you and all other men having regard to the whole of your future life, and I myself in the prospect of death. For at this moment I am sensible that I have not the temper of a philosopher; like the vulgar, I am only a partisan. Now the partisan, when he is engaged in a dispute, cares nothing about the rights of the question, but is anxious only to convince his hearers of his own assertions. And the difference between him and me at the present moment is merely this—that whereas he seeks to convince his hearers that what he says is true, I am rather seeking to convince myself. . . . And I would ask you to be thinking of the truth and not of Socrates: agree with me, if I seem to you to be speaking the truth; or if not, withstand me might and main, that I may not deceive you as well as myself in my enthusiasm, and like the bee, leave my sting in you before I die.

Plato : *Phaedo* (trans. B. Jowett)

Your letter, most learned Erasmus, as it is very long, so also is it most eloquent and happy. It is a proof of a tenacious memory and gives a faithful review of our discussion. . . . But it contains nothing to alter or detract from the opinions which I imbibed from St. Jerome. Not that I am perverse and obstinate with an uncandid pertinacity, but that (though I may be mistaken) I think I hold and defend the truth, or what is most like the truth . . . I am unwilling, just now, to grapple with your letter as a whole; for I have neither leisure nor strength to do so at once, and without preparation. But I will attack the first part of it—your first line of battle as it were. . . . In the meantime do you patiently hear me, and let us both, if, when striking our flints together, any spark should fly out, eagerly catch at it. For we seek, not for victory in argument, but for truth, which perchance may be elicited by the clash of argument with argument, as sparks are by the clashing of steel against steel!

John Colet: *Letters*

No one will be better satisfied than I to see Mr. Darwin's book refuted, if any person be competent to perform that feat; but I would suggest that refutation is retarded, not aided, by mere sarcastic misrepresentation. . . . The question is one to be settled only by the painstaking truth-loving investigation of skilled naturalists. It is the duty of the general public to await the result in patience; and above all things, to discourage, as they would any other crimes, the attempt to enlist the prejudices of the ignorant, or the uncharitableness of the bigoted, on either side of the controversy.

Finally, one word for myself, I have not hesitated to speak strongly where I have felt strongly; and I am but too conscious that the indicative and imperative moods have too often taken the place of the more becoming subjunctive and conditional. I feel, therefore, how necessary it is to beg you to forget the personality of him who has thus ventured to address you, and to consider only the truth or error in what has been said.

Thomas Huxley: *Addresses*

It is characteristic of indifference that it is either totally cynical or, more often, limited to certain fields and coupled with reckless intolerance in some others. . . . Indifference has not the power to fill a whole human being; true tolerance, however, is all round or it is not true tolerance. . . .

When describing tolerance as a total attitude, I do not mean a superficial, indiscriminate friendliness to everybody and everything, accompanied by a great reluctance to express any opinions of one's own. . . . Like indifference [this] is an early stage of intolerance, at least when it is based on the silent assumption that, while I am big enough to bear with another's belief, he may possibly be less tolerant to mine. This is another way of taking our neighbour not seriously enough. . . . It is as intolerant to suppress one's own glimpse of truth as that of another person.

Richard K. Ullmann: *Tolerance and the Intolerable*

It is important to note that from the very beginning of the Reformation controversies, there were individuals who pressed the case for freedom of conscience precisely on religious grounds. And though the establishment of toleration in the world may owe much to the man for whom religion was a matter of comparative indifference, the basic argument for religious liberty has always had to find its roots in the nature of religion itself. Precisely because religion was supremely important, it came to be held that one man could not impose it upon an individual. . . . Mere religious indifference is not sufficient to create or preserve freedom. The important moment comes when the man who holds his religion as an absolute realises from this very fact that he must respect what the other man equally considers to be absolute.

Herbert Butterfield: *The Historical Development of the Principle of Toleration in British Life*

We commonly shunne correction whereas we should rather seeke and present our selves unto it, chiefly when it commeth by the way of conference, and not of regency. At every opposition, we consider not whether it be just; but be it right or wrong, how we may avoide it: Instead of reaching our armes, we stretch forth our clawes unto it. I should endure to bee rudely handled and checked by my friends, though they should call me foole, coxecombe, or say I raved. I love a man that doth stoutly expresse himselfe, amongst honest and worthy men, and whose words answere his thoughts. We should fortifie and harden our hearing, against the tendernesse of the ceremonious sound of words. I love a friendly society and a virile and constant familiarity.

Montaigne: *Essays.* Third Book, Chapter VIII (trans. Florio)

Description of a Gentleman

Nowhere shall we find greater candour, consideration, indulgence: he throws himself into the minds of his opponents, he accounts for their mistakes. He knows the weakness of human reason as well as its strength, its province and its limits. If he be an unbeliever, he will be too profound and large-minded to ridicule religion or to act against it; he is too wise to be a dogmatist or fanatic in his infidelity. He respects piety and devotion; he even supports institutions as venerable, beautiful, or useful, to which he does not assent; he honours the ministers of religion, and it contents him to decline its mysteries without assailing or denouncing them. He is a friend of religious toleration, and that, not only because his philosophy has taught him to look on all forms of faith with an impartial eye, but also from the gentleness and effeminacy of feeling, which is the attendant on civilization.

Newman: *The Idea of a University*

There cannot be greater Rudeness, than to interrupt another in the current of his Discourse; for if there be not impertinent Folly in answering a Man before we know what he will say, yet it is a plain Declaration, that we are weary to hear him talk any longer: And have a Disesteem of what he says, which we judging not fit to entertain the Company, desire them to give Audience to us, who have something to produce worth their Attention. . . . To which, if there be added, as is usual, a correcting of any Mistake, or a contradiction of what has been said, 'tis a Mark of yet greater Pride and Self-conceitedness. . . .

I do not say this that I think there should be no Differences of Opinions in Conversation, nor Opposition in Men's Discourses: This would be to take away the greatest Advantage of Society and the Improvements are to be made by ingenious Company; where the light is to be got from the opposite Arguings of Men of Parts, shewing the different Sides of things . . . 'Tis not the owning ones Dissent from another, that I speak against, but the manner of doing it.

Locke: *On Education*

A discourteous Knight

GLENDOWER

Three times hath Henry Bolingbroke made head
Against my power; thrice from the banks of Wye
And sandy-bottom'd Severn have I sent him
Bootless home and weather beaten back.

HOTSPUR

Home without boots, and in foul weather too!
How scapes he agues, in the devil's name?

GLENDOWER

Come, here's the map: shall we divide our right
According to our threefold order ta'en?

MORTIMER

The archdeacon hath divided it
Into three limits very equally.

★

HOTSPUR

Methinks my moiety, north from Burton here,
In quantity equals not one of yours:

See how this river comes me cranking in,
And cuts me from the best of all my land
A huge half-moon, a monstrous cantle out
I'll have the current in this place damm'd up.
And here the smug and silver Trent shall run
In a new channel, fair and evenly:
It shall not wind with such a deep indent,
To rob me of so rich a bottom here.

GLENDOWER

Not wind! It shall, it must, you see it doth.

*

HOTSPUR

I'll have it so; a little charge will do it.

GLENDOWER

I will not have it alter'd.

HOTSPUR

Will not you?

GLENDOWER

No, nor you shall not.

HOTSPUR

Who shall say me nay?

GLENDOWER

Why, that will I.

HOTSPUR

Let me not understand you then
Speak it in Welsh.

GLENDOWER

I can speak English, Lord, as well as you,
For I was train'd up in the English court;
Where, being but young, I framed to the harp
Many an English ditty lovely well,
And gave the tongue an helpful ornament;
A virtue that was never seen in you.

HOTSPUR

Marry, and I'm glad of it with all my heart.
I had rather be a kitten, and cry mew

Than one of these same metre ballad-mongers;
I had rather hear a brazen can stick turn'd
Or a dry wheel grate on the axle-tree;
And that would set my teeth nothing on edge
Nothing so much as mincing poetry;
Tis like the forc'd gait of a shuffling nag.

GLENDOWER

Come, you shall have Trent turn'd.

HOTSPUR

I do not care: I'll give thrice so much land
To any well-deserving friend;
But in the way of bargain, mark you me,
I'll cavil on the ninth part of a hair.
Are the Indentures drawn? Shall we be gone?

GLENDOWER

The moon shines fair, you may away by night:
I'll haste the writer and withal
Break with your wives of your departure hence: . . . [exit

MORTIMER

Fie, cousin Percy! how you cross my father!

*

HOTSPUR

O! he's as tedious
As a tired horse, a railing wife;
Worse than a smoky house. I had rather live
With cheese and garlick in a windmill, far,
Than feed on cates and have him talk to me
In any summer-house in Christendom.

MORTIMER

In faith, he is a worthy gentleman,
Exceeding well read and profited
In strange concealments, valiant as a lion
And wondrous affable, and as bountiful
As mines of India. Shall I tell you, cousin?
He holds your temper in a high respect,
And curbs himself even of his natural scope

When you do cross his humour; faith, he does
I warrant you, that man is not alive
Might so have tempted him as you have done,
Without the taste of danger and reproof:
But do not use it oft, let me entreat you.

WORCESTER

In faith, my lord, you are too wilful blame;
And since your coming hither have done enough
To put him quite beside his patience.
You must needs learn, lord, to amend this fault.
Though sometimes it showes greatness, courage, blood,—
And that's the dearest grace it renders you,—
Yet oftentimes it doth present harsh rage,
Defect of manners, want of government,
Pride, haughtiness, opinion and disdain:
The least of which haunting a nobleman
Loseth men's hearts and leaves behind a stain
Upon the beauty of all parts besides,
Beguiling them of commendation.

Shakespeare: *Henry IV*, Part I. Act III, Scene 1

A courteous Knight

A Knight there was and that a worthy man,
That from the tyme that he first bigan
To riden out, he lovéd chivalrie,
Trouthe and honour, freedom and curteisie,

*

And though that he were worthy, he was wys,
And of his port as meeke as is a mayde.
He never yet no vileyne ne sayde,
In al his lyf, unto no maner wight
He was a verray parfit gentil knyght.

Chaucer: *Prologue to Canterbury Tales*

[Letter from Lord Holland about his uncle Charles James Fox.]

It is rather odd that he is more republican than me in France and I more than him in England. But surely it must increase my respect for his character as well as my exteem for his person, that he hears with the greatest tolerance and good nature all my arguments and opinions; and he is the only man I ever met with who, when he has a decided superiority in talents and in experience, puts himself upon an equality and fights from a level without an appearance of affectation or condescension.

Lord Holland: *Memorials & Correspondence*

The wise and good man neither strives with any himself, nor in the measure of his power will he allow another to strive. And in this, as in all other things, the life of Socrates is set before us as an example; who did not only himself fly all contention, but also forbade it to others. See in Xenophon's Symposium how many quarrels he ended; and, again, how he bore with Thrasymachus, and how with Polus and with Callictes; and how he enduced his wife, and how his son, which opposed him with sophistical arguments. For he remembered very well that no man can command the ruling faculty of another.

Epictetus on Socrates

As life advances, a more modest, a calmer, sweeter, more tolerant spirit begins to infuse itself into a man's mind. . . . Seeing in all churches men whose lives breathe the very spirit of Christ shall he turn away with unchristian hardness and exclusiveness from men whom he may soon have to meet in heaven? . . . Let us recall to mind the good and holy men of different sects and churches who once were with us and ask whether the points which divided them here, and about which they contended and wrangled so hotly, can keep them asunder there, in that deeper, diviner life into which they have entered.

John Caird: *University Sermons*

I cannot fall out, or contemn a man for an error, or conceive why a difference in opinion should divide an affection: for controversies, disputes, and argumentations, both in philosophy and in divinity, if they meet with discreet and peaceable natures, do not infringe the laws of charity: in all disputes, so much as there is of passion, so much there is of nothing to the purpose; for then reason, like a bad hound, spends upon a false scent, and forsakes the question first started. And this is one reason why controversies are never determined; for though they be amply proposed, they are scarce at all handled, they do so swell with unnecessary disgressions; and the parenthesis on the party is often as large as the main discourse upon the subject.

Sir Thomas Browne: *Religio Medici*

Indeed some charitable Divines have counted it inconsistent with the lenity of the Gospel, which is to expect and endeavour the amendment of all, to put any to death for their false opinions; and we read of S Paul (though the Papists paint him alwayes with a sword) that he onely came with a rod.

Thomas Fuller

You shall not finde a Trismegistus, a Numa Pompilius, a Plato, a Socrates, for whose salvation you shall not finde some Father, or some Ancient and Reverend Author, an Advocate . . . and partly they goe upon that rule, which goes through so many of the Fathers, *Facienti quod in se est*, That to that man who does as much as he can, by the light of nature, God never denies grace; and then, say they, why should not these men that doe so be saved? I know God can be as mercifull as those tender Fathers present him to be; and I would be as charitable as they are. And therefore humbly imbracing that manifestation of his Son, which he hath afforded me, I leave God, to his unsearchable waies of working upon others, without farther inquisition.

John Donne: *Sermons*

However, one must never confuse error and the person who errs, not even when there is question of error or inadequate knowledge of truth in the moral or religious field. The person who errs is always and above all a human being, and he retains in every case his dignity as a human person; and he must be always regarded and treated in accordance with that lofty dignity. Besides, in every human being, there is a need that is congenital to his nature and never becomes extinguished, compelling him to break through the web of error and open his mind to the knowledge of truth. And God will never fail to act on his interior being, with the result that a person, who at a given moment of his life lacks the clarity of faith or even adheres to erroneous doctrines, can at a future date be enlightened and believe the truth. Meetings and agreements, in the various sectors of daily life, between believers and those who do not believe or believe insufficiently because they adhere to error, can be occasions for discovering truth and paying homage to it.

Pope John XXIII: *Pacem in Terris*

Whilst the mercies of God do promise us heaven, our conceits and opinions exclude us from that place. There must be therefore more than one St. Peter. Particular churches and sects usurp the gates of heaven, and turn the key against each other: and thus we go to heaven against each other's wills, conceits, and opinions, and, with as much uncharity as ignorance, do err, I fear, in points not only of our own, but one another's salvation.

I believe many are saved, who to man seem reprobated; and many are reprobated, who in the opinion and sentence of man stand elected. There will appear at the last day strange and unexpected examples, both of his justice and his mercy; and therefore to define either is folly in man, and insolency even in the devils.

Sir Thomas Browne: *Religio Medici*

God sees not as man sees, chooses not as man chooses, lest we should devote our selves again to set places and assemblies and outward callings of men, planting our faith one while in the old Convocation House, and another while in the Chappell at Westminster; when all the faith and religion that shall be there canoniz'd is not sufficient, without plain convincement and the charity of patient instruction, to supple the least bruise of conscience, to edifie the meanest Christian, who desires to walk in the Spirit, and not in the letter of human trust, for all the number of voices that can be there made; no, though Harry the 7 himself there, with all his liege tombs about him, should lend them voices from the dead, to swell their number. And if the men be erroneous who appear to be the leading schismaticks, what withholds us but our sloth, our self-will, and distrust in the right cause, that we doe not give them gentle meetings and gentle dismissions, that we debate not and examin the matter throughly with liberall and frequent audience; if not for their sakes, yet for our own, seeing no man who hath tasted learning, but will confesse the many waies of profiting by those who not contented with stale receits are able to manage and set forth new positions to the world? And were they but as the dust and cinders of our feet, so long as in that notion they may serve to polish and brighten the armoury of Truth, ev'n for that respect they were not utterly to be cast away. But if they be of those whom God hath fitted for the speciall use of these times with eminent and ample gifts, and those perhaps neither among the Priests nor among the Pharisees, and we in the hast of a precipitant zeal shall make no distinction, but resolve to stop their mouths because we fear they come with new and dangerous opinions, as we commonly forejudge them ere we understand them, no lesse then woe to us, while, thinking thus to defend the Gospel, we are found the persecutors.

John Milton: *Areopagitica*

It is not the unfrocking of a Priest, the unmitring of a Bishop, and the removing him from off the Presbyterian shoulders that will make us a happy Nation; . . . There be who perpetually complain of schisms and sects and make it such a calamity that any man dissents from their maxims. 'Tis their own pride and ignorance which causes the disturbing, who neither will hear with meekness nor can convince; yet all must be supprest which is not found in their Syntagma. . . . Under these fantastic terrors of sect and schism, we wrong the earnest and zealous thirst after knowledge and understanding which God hath stirr'd up in this City. . . . A little generous prudence, a little forbearance of one another and som grain of charity might win all these diligences to joyn and unite in one generall and brotherly search after Truth.

John Milton: *Areopagitica*

[Letter to General Assembly of the Kirk of Scotland.]

Only give me leave to say, in a word: you take upon you to judge us in the things of our God, though you know us not; . . . And by your hard and subtle words you have begotten prejudice in those who do too much . . . depend upon you . . . I am persuaded that divers of you who lead the people have laboured to build yourselves in these things wherein you have censured others, and established yourselves upon the Word of God. Is it therefore infallibly agreeable to the Word of God, all that you say? I beseech you, in the bowels of Christ, think it possible you may be mistaken. . . .

I pray you read the 28th of Isaiah from the fifth to the fifteenth "verse". And do not scorn to know that it is the Spirit that quickens and giveth life.

The Lord give you and us understanding to do that which is well-pleasing in His sight.

Committing you to the grace of God, I rest
Your humble servant,
Oliver Cromwell

I now see that good men are not so good as I once thought they were, but have more imperfections . . . and I find that few are so bad as either their malicious enemies or censorious separating professors do imagine. . . . I am not so much inclined to pass a peremptory sentence of damnation upon all that never heard of Christ, having some more reason than I knew of before to think that God's dealing with such is much unknown to us, and that the ungodly here among us Christians are in a far worse case than they.

My censures of Papists do much differ from what they were at first . . . now I doubt not but that God hath many sanctified ones among them who have received the true doctrine of Christ so practically that their contradictory errors prevail not against them to hinder their love of God and their salvation. . . . And I can never believe that a man may not be saved by that religion which doth but bring him to the true love of God and to a heavenly mind. . . . And I am assured too that the Papists' mis-expressions and mis-understanding us with our mistaking of them and inconvenient expressing our own opinions hath made our differences to appear much greater than they are.

. . . I am deeplier afflicted for the disagreements of Christians than when I was younger . . . nothing is so sad and grievous to my thoughts as the case of divided Churches. The contentions between the Greek Church and the Roman, the Papists and the Protestants, the Lutherans and the Calvinists, have woefully hindered the Kingdom of Christ. . . . I cannot be of that opinion that think God will not accept him that prayeth by the Common Prayer Book nor yet can I be of their mind that say the like of extemporary prayer: . . . Alas! while we wrangle here in the dark, we are all dying and passing to the world that will decide all our controversies and the safest passage thither is by peaceable holiness.

Richard Baxter: *Autobiography*

We think it best that there be no provision to promote uniformity in matters of religion, except a perfect freedom of inquiry . . . if the disputants come to no agreement in opinion, they will all of them have an opportunity of acquiring the divine principle of universal charity with respect to those that differ from them.

Joseph Priestley: *Tracts relating to the Dissenters*

When [the] mystery of divine love was first manifested to the world it produced its proper effects, it put an end to all selfishness and division; for all that believed were of one heart, and one spirit, and had all things in common. . . . But now it is so difficult to enter into controversy without being, or at least seeming, in some degree unkind to the person that one opposes, that it is with great reluctance that I have entered upon my present undertaking; having nothing more deeply riveted in my heart than an universal love and kindness for all mankind, and more especially for those whom God has called to be my fellow-labourers in promoting the salvation of mankind. But however unwilling, yet I find myself obliged to consider and lay open many grievous faults in the doctor's discourse . . . And this I must do with great plainness and sincerity, in the love of truth, and under the direction of charity saying nothing in the spirit of an adversary, sparing nothing through respect of persons, sacrificing nothing to the taste or temper of the world, but setting forth everything in that naked light in which the Spirit of God represents it to my own mind.

William Law: *Two Answers to Dr. Trapp*

As for me, I keep myself as far as possible neutral, the better to assist the new flowering of good learning; and it seems to me that more can be done by unassuming courteousness than by violence. It was thus that Christ brought the world under His sway, and thus that Paul made away with the Jewish Law, by interpreting all things allegorically. It is wiser to cry out against those who abuse the Pope's authority than against the Popes themselves, and I think we should act in the same way with the Kings. As for the schools, we should not so much reject them as recall them to more reasonable studies. Where things are too generally accepted to be suddenly eradicated from men's minds, we must argue with repeated and efficacious proofs and not make positive assertions. The poisonous contentions of certain persons are better ignored than refuted. We must everywhere take care never to speak or act arrogantly or in a party spirit: this I believe is pleasing to the Spirit of Christ. Meanwhile we must preserve our minds from being seduced by anger, hatred, or ambition; these feelings are apt to lie in wait for us in the midst of our strivings after piety.

Erasmus to Luther: *Letters*

I cannot laugh at, but rather pity the fruitless journeys of pilgrims, or contemn the miserable condition of friars; for though misplaced in circumstances, there is something in it of devotion. I could never hear the Ave Maria bell without an elevation, or think it a sufficient warrant, because they erred in one circumstance, for me to err in all, that is, in silence and dumb contempt; whilst therefore they direct their devotions to her, I offer mine to God, and rectify the errors of their prayers, by rightly ordering mine own. At a solemn procession I have wept abundantly, while my consorts, blind with opposition and prejudice, have fallen into an excess of scorn and laughter.

Sir Thomas Browne: *Religio Medici*

Idols were carefully made by the heathen in the error of their hands rather than their minds.

John of Salisbury

Let no one despise another because his manner of life is different. ... In every path of life let all strive to attain to the mind of Christ (*scopum Christi*). Let us assist one another, neither envying those who surpass us, nor despising those who may lag behind. And if any one should excel another, let him beware lest he be like the Pharisee in the Gospel, who recounted his good deeds to God; rather let him follow the teaching of Christ, and say, "I am an unprofitable servant". No one more truly has faith than he who distrusts himself. No one is really further from true religion than he who thinks himself most religious.

Erasmus: *Preface to the Enchiridon*

Since therefore it is unavoidable to the greatest part of men, if not all, to have several opinions, without certain and indubitable proof of their truths; ... it would methinks become all men to maintain peace and the common offices of humanity and friendship, in the diversity of opinions. ... We should do well to commiserate our mutual ignorance, and endeavour to remove it in all the gentle and fair ways of information; not instantly treat others ill, as obstinate and perverse, because they will not renounce their own, and receive our opinions.

John Locke: *On Education*

If we can imagine Shelley and Queen Victoria arguing out their differences in another world, we may be sure that the Queen has long ago found out that she cannot settle the question by classing Shelley with George IV as a bad man; and Shelley is not likely to have called her vile names on the general ground that as the economic dependence of women makes marriage a money bargain in which the man is the purchaser and the woman the purchased, there is no essential difference between a married woman and the woman of the streets.

George Bernard Shaw: Preface to *Getting Married*

There is such a thing as stereoscopic thinking—the viewing subjects as well as objects with our two eyes. Some men of intense nature shut one of the eyes of the mind, because then there is a straight line between his eye and object; but for the whereabouts and relations of a subject, it is well to look with both eyes; and so it comes to pass that the focus of one man's mental vision differs from that of another, probably in some respects from that of all others, and hence the allowance which we should make for other men when they fail to see not only things, but thoughts, exactly as we do. We will find, when we look through their stereoscope, we don't see their image as they do—it may be double, it may be distorted and blurred.

John Brown: *Horae Subsecivae*

[Andrew Marvell's *Horatian Ode*, though written in Cromwell's honour, contains a fine tribute to Charles I.]

Then burning through the air he went
And palaces and temples rent;
And Caesar's head at last
Did through his laurels blast.

Tis madness to resist or blame
The face of angry Heaven's flame;
And if we would speak true,
Much to the man is due

Who, from his private gardens, where
He lived reservéd and austere
As if his highest plot
To plant the bergamot

Could by industrious valour climb
To ruin the great work of time,
And cast the kingdoms old
Into another mould;

★

That thence the Royal actor borne
The tragic scaffold might adorn:
While round the arméd bands
Did clap their bloody hands.

He nothing common did or mean
Upon that memorable scene,
But with his keener eye
The axe's edge did try,

Nor call'd the gods, with vulgar spite
To vindicate his helpless right;
But bow'd his comely head
Down, as upon a bed.

The freedom which we enjoy in our government extends also to our ordinary life. There, far from exercising a jealous surveillance over each other, we do not feel called upon to be angry with our neighbour for doing what he likes, or even to indulge in those injurious looks which cannot fail to be offensive, although they inflict no positive penalty.

Thucydides

Loth to obey, loth to command . . . convention alone has forced me to be anywhere a master. Ariel and Caliban, had I been Prospero on that island, would have had nothing to do and nothing to complain of; and Man Friday on that other island would have bored me, had I been Crusoe. When I was a King in Babylon and you were a Christian slave, I promptly freed you. Anarchistic? Yes; and I have no defence to offer, except the rather lame one that I am a Tory Anarchist. I should like every one to go about doing just as he pleased—short of altering any of the things to which I have grown accustomed.

Max Beerbohm: *And Even Now*

I am convinced it is a great art to know how to grow old gracefully, and I desire to practise it. One secret of it I am sure is to take the side of the young people, and I mean to do this just as far as possible. When I remember my own youth, and recall the immense power any old person, who believed in me and sympathised with me, had over me in those days, I cannot but think my influence for good over the young people of my day will be far greater by the road of sympathy than by the road of antagonism.

Mrs. Pearsall Smith: *Letters*

We have been to see our neighbour at Blackdown, Lord Tennyson, who is now 83 years of age. I have always been devoted to his "In Memoriam" but I find that it is not the fashion with the most artistic young people of the present generation to admire Tennyson. They even declare he is not a poet in the true sense of the word at all! I should be dreadfully shocked at this, only that I remember how in my young days I scorned the poetry which the generation before me admired, such as Cowper and Dryden . . . I cannot keep up with the coming generation in their literary taste, but it is very interesting to hear all about it. And I confess I enjoy seeing them have opinions of their own. The individual human being is a wonderful thing to my mind, and everything that reveals it interests me immensely.

Mrs. Pearsall Smith: *Letters*

Certainly the limits of adorning and beautifying the body are not so narrow, so strict, as by some sowre men they are sometimes conceived to be. Differences of Ranks, of Ages, of Nations, of Customes, make great differences in the enlarging, or contracting of these limits, in adorning the body; and that may come neare sin at some time, and in some places, which is not so alwaies, nor every where. Amongst the women there, the Jewish women, it was so generall a thing to helpe themselves with aromaticall Oyles, and liniments, as that that which is said by the Prophets poore Widow, to the Prophet Elisha, That she had nothing in the house but a pot of Oyle, is very properly by some collected from the Originall word, that it was not Oyle for meate, but Oyle for unction, aromaticall Oyle, Oyle to make her looke better; she was but poore, but a Widow, but a Prophets Widow, (and likely to be the poorer for that) yet she left not that. We see that even those women, whom the Kings were to take for their Wives, and not for Mistresses, (which is but a later name for Concubines) had a certaine, and a long time assigned to be prepared by these aromaticall unctions, and liniments for beauty.

John Donne: *Sermons*

Letters to her daughter

I send thee a belated birthday present—a telescope Cigarette holder. Thee need not advertise that it is a present from the author of the "Christian's Secret of a Happy Life"!

Feb. 22, 1906.

I do not wonder thee was "jiggered" over that cigarette case. I felt rather jiggered myself. But as thee is too old for me to forbid thee to smoke, and so I am entirely delivered from responsibility, I want, since thee will smoke, to help thee to do it as comfortably as possible. I do not understand it, unless it is that the mother in me gets the better of the reformer sometimes! And I happened to see that little holder at one of those moments. Such are the frailties of poor human nature!

Mrs. Pearsall Smith

THIRD PART

CHARITY

The open mind makes possible the practice of tolerance in the full acceptance of life, and that acceptance faces us eventually with the question how to meet evil, that evil which cannot be tolerated. The answer is with sacrificial love. The relation of tolerance to charity is fundamental, there can be no true tolerance without it. It is charity that saves us on the one hand from indifference and cynicism and on the other from intolerance. And only through love can we be strong enough to meet that denial of humanity in ourselves and in others which can never be tolerated but must somehow be redeemed. "Charity suffereth long and is kind—Charity envieth not, charity vaunteth not itself, is not puffed up . . . is not easily provoked, thinketh no evil, rejoiceth not in iniquity but rejoiceth in the truth. Beareth all things, believeth all things, hopeth all things, endureth all things." (Cor. I, xiii)

I

Charity towards the Weak and Exploited

Subject races and countries—the poor—prisoners
minority sects—women—children

Blessed are the merciful.

St. Matthew

There is no caste in blood, which runneth in one hue
Nor caste in tears, which trickle salt withal.

Attributed to Buddha

No one is born prejudiced against others: but everyone is born prejudiced in favour of himself.

D. Stafford-Clark

[To give some impression of the climate of opinion within which tolerance constantly had to struggle, here are a few intolerant assertions by influential writers. These are representative of views widely held on the weak and exploited classes defended by the tolerant.]

Thomas Carlyle addressing the Negroes (1853)

Quashee, if he will not help in bringing out the spices, will get himself made a slave again . . . and with beneficent whip, since other methods avail not, will be compelled to work. You are not slaves now; nor do I wish, if it can be avoided, to see you slaves again: but decidedly you have to be servants to those who are born wiser than you; that you may depend upon, my obscure black friends—that are born Lords of you—Servants to the Whites if they are (as what mortal man can doubt they are?) born wiser than you!

Bernard Mandeville upon the poor (18th century)

Men who are to remain and end their days in a Laborious, Tiresome and Painful Station of Life, the sooner they are put upon it at first, the more patiently they'll submit to it for ever after.

Lord Brougham upon the starving Irish

In March 1846, when the Irish famine was becoming desperate and hundreds of impoverished tenants, unable to pay their rents, were being evicted Lord Brougham said—"Undoubtedly it was the landlord's right to do as he pleased, and if he abstained he conferred a favour and was doing an act of kindness. If on the other hand he chose to stand on his right, the tenants must be taught by the strong arm of the law that they had no power to oppose or resist."

The Greville Memoirs for 12 Dec., 1846

[The Irish are] a people with rare exceptions besotted with obstinacy and indolence, reckless and savage—all from high to low intent on doing as little and getting as much as they can. . . . There is no doubt that the people never were so well off on the whole as they have been this year of famine.

The Morning Post on the Roman Catholic Relief Bill, 1829

There never was an admission more distinct and unequivocal than that which is to be gathered from the conduct and language of Mr. Apostate Peel and his supporters in the House of Commons, that the revolutionary measure they are determined to force upon the country is obnoxious and revolting to the public mind. . . . We have on the side of the Constitution every man who dare claim for himself the title of a high authority in the laws of the land . . . And what is there to oppose this? A host of infidels, Republicans, Papists, Savoyards, Bourbonists . . . all without exception alien to the Nation.

Martin Luther on women

If a woman becomes weary or at last dead from bearing, that matters not; let her only die from bearing, she is there to do it.

Rousseau upon women in their relation to men

The education of women should always be relative to that of men. To please, to be useful to us, to make us love and esteem them, to educate us when young and take care of us when grown up, to advise, to console us, to render our lives easy and agreeable, these are the duties of women at all times, and what they should be taught in their infancy.

Lady Mary Wortley Montague on the learned among her own sex

There is hardly a character in the world more despicable, or more liable to universal ridicule than that of a learned woman.

Canon Butler's advice to parents

"Break your child's will early, or he will break yours later on."

Advertisement from The Times of Feb. 16, 1864.

Boarding Schools Wanted, in London, for a boy, nine years, and two girls, six and seven years old, requiring firm discipline. . . . No holyday could be given, as holydays destroy any good effected at school.

Climbing Boys

Lord Beaumont declared Shaftesbury's Bill to prohibit the employment of climbing chimney sweep children to be "a pitiful cant of pseudo-philanthropy".

"For he is our peace, who made both one, and brake down the middle-wall of partition, having abolished in his flesh the enmity" (Ephesians II, 14, 15).

When St. Paul set out to review the function of the Church in the Purpose of God, in the Epistle to the Ephesians, he laid it down as the Church's great task that it should create unity among men. There was in the world of his experience one great division, the division between Jew and Gentile, symbolised by the wall of partition which marked the inner boundary of the Court of the Gentiles in the Jewish Temple and which bore the inscription—"If any man of another race passes this boundary, he has only himself to thank if his death ensues." St. Paul saw that this great division had become quite unimportant. It was inconceivable that the Love of God, as Jesus understood it, should be limited to a single race. The manifestation of the Love of God which He had given had broken down the middle wall of partition.

But He has done more than this: He has "abolished enmity in His flesh". What does this mean?

There is no way by which we may be sure of bringing men into harmony with one another except by bringing both into allegiance to the will of God. The Purpose of God includes the welfare of all, and nothing else does that; and therefore it is only in obedience to that Purpose that we all find ourselves united and harmonious.

William Temple: *Sermons*

First among the rules governing the relations between States is that of truth. This calls, above all, for the elimination of every trace of racialism, and the consequent recognition of the principle that all States are by nature equal in dignity. Each of them accordingly is vested with the right to existence, to self-development, to the means fitting to its attainment, and to be the one primarily responsible for this self-development. Add to that the right of each to its good name, and to the respect which is its due. Very often, experience has taught us, individuals will be found to differ considerably, in knowledge, virtue, talent and wealth. Yet these inequalities must never be held to excuse any man's attempt to lord it over his neighbours unjustly. They constitute rather a source of greater responsibility in the contribution which each and everyone must make towards mutual improvement.

Similarly, political communities may have reached different levels of culture, civilization or economic development. Neither is that a sufficient reason for some to take unjust advantage of their superiority over others; rather should they see in it an added motive for more serious commitment to the common cause of social progress.

It is not true that some human beings are by nature superior, and others inferior. All men are equal in their natural dignity. Consequently there are no political communities which are superior by nature and none which are inferior by nature. All political communities are of equal natural dignity, since they are bodies whose membership is made up of these same human beings. Nor must it be forgotten, in this connection, that peoples can be highly sensitive, and with good reason, in matters touching their dignity and honour.

★

There are groupings of people of more or less different racial backgrounds. However, the elements which characterize an ethnic group must not be transformed into a watertight compartment in which human beings are prevented from communicating with their fellow men belonging to different ethnic groups. That would contrast with our contemporary situation, in which the distances separating peoples have been almost wiped out. Nor can one overlook the fact that, even though human beings differ from one another by virtue of their ethnic peculiarities, they all possess certain essential common elements, and are inclined by nature to meet each other in the world of spiritual values, whose progressive assimilation opens to them the possibility of perfection without limits. They have the right and duty therefore to live in communion with one another.

Pope John XXIII: *Pacem in Terris*

Racial segregation is a temporal behaviour which assumes that it has cancelled the eternal fact of the oneness of man; it separates on the social, or economic, or civil level that which cannot be separated in the deeper reaches of the human soul. And the result for White man and Negro is an illness, the illness of those who are estranged from those to whom they belong. For however fine we may draw out the nerve which connects man to man, it does not break. If it did, all the agonies, the aches and sorrows of human separation would break with it; but it does not break; it holds forever, thin and taut; and along this nerve throb the anxieties, the fears, the pangs of human estrangement.

From the anxieties of this separation the White man has in the past tried to escape, not by restoring and completing the broken union, but by seeking to make the severance complete.

Kyle Haselden: *The Racial Problem in Christian Perspective*

[In 1954, when the Supreme Court of the U.S.A. pronounced separate schools for white and negro children to be unconstitutional, Chief Justice Warren said:]

To separate negro children from others of similar age and qualifications solely because of their race generates a feeling of inferiority as to their stakes in the community that may affect their hearts and minds in a way unlikely ever to be undone.

My mother bore me in the southern wild,
And I am black; but oh, my soul is white!
White as an angel is the English child,
But I am black, as if bereaved of light.

My mother taught me underneath a tree,
And, sitting down before the heat of day,
She took me on her lap and kissèd me,
And, pointing to the East, began to say:

"Look on the rising sun: there God does live,
And gives His light, and gives His heat away,
And flowers and trees and beasts and men receive
Comfort in morning, joy in the noonday.

"And we are put on earth a little space,
That we may learn to bear the beams of love,
And these black bodies and this sunburnt face
Are but a cloud, and like a shady grove.

"For, when our souls have learned the heat to bear,
The cloud will vanish, we shall hear His voice,
Saying, 'Come out from the grove, My love and care,
And round My golden tent like lambs rejoice.' "

Thus did my mother say, and kissèd me,
And thus I say to little English boy.
When I from black, and he from white cloud free,
And round the tent of God like lambs we joy,

I'll shade him from the heat till he can bear
To lean in joy upon our Father's knee;
And then I'll stand and stroke his silver hair,
And be like him, and he will then love me.

William Blake: *The Little Black Boy*

[In *Sandford & Merton*, the famous Victorian children's educational manual, the author Thomas Day, who was one of the earliest abolitionists, tried, in the form of a Socratic dialogue, to convince Tommy of the evils of slavery. Tommy's father was a rich slave owner.]

MR. BARLOW "And what right have the people who sold the poor negroes to your father to sell them, or what right has your father to buy them?" Here Tommy seemed a good deal puzzled, but at length he said: "They are brought from a country that is a great way off, in ships, and so become slaves."

MR. BARLOW "Then, if I take you to another country in a ship I shall have the right to sell you?"

TOMMY "No, but you won't, sir, because I was born a gentleman."

MR. BARLOW "What do you mean by that, Tommy?"

TOMMY (a little confounded) "Why to have a fine house and fine clothes, and a coach, and a great deal of money, as my papa has."

MR. BARLOW "Then if you were no longer to have a fine house, nor fine clothes, nor a great deal of money, somebody that had all these things might make you a slave, and use you ill, and beat you and insult you, and do whatever he liked with you?"

TOMMY "No, sir, that would not be right, neither, that anybody should use me ill."

MR. BARLOW "Then one person should not use another ill?"

TOMMY "No, sir."

MR. BARLOW "To make a slave of anybody is to use him ill, is it not?"

TOMMY "I think so."

MR. BARLOW "Then no one ought to make a slave of you?"

TOMMY "No, indeed, sir."

MR. BARLOW "But if no one should use another ill, and making a slave is using him ill, neither ought you to make a slave of anyone else."

TOMMY "Indeed, sir, I think not."

Placing on men the ignominious title slave, dressing them in uncomely garments, keeping them to servile labour, in which they are often dirty, tends gradually to fix a notion in the mind that they are a sort of people below us in nature . . . And moreover a person which in our esteem is mean and contemptible, if their language or behaviour toward us is unseemly or disrespectful, it excites wrath more powerfully than the like conduct in one we accounted our equal or superior; and, where this happens to be the case, it disqualifies for candid judgement. For it is unfit for a person to sit as judge in a case where his own personal resentments are stirred up.

John Woolman: *Some Considerations on the Keeping of Negroes*

President Kennedy's Address on Civil Rights

This nation was founded by men of many nations and backgrounds. It was founded on the principle that all men are created equal, and that the rights of every man are diminished when the rights of one man are threatened . . . It ought to be possible for every American to enjoy the privileges of being American without regard to his race or his colour. In short every American ought to have the right to be treated as he would wish to be treated, as one would wish his children to be treated. But this is not the case. The Negro baby born in America today, regardless of the section of the nation in which he is born, has about one half as much chance of completing high school as a white baby born in the same place on the same day; one third as much chance of completing college; one third as much chance of becoming a professional man, twice as much chance of becoming unemployed; . . . a life expectancy which is seven years shorter, and the prospects of earning only half as much.

This is not a sectional issue. Men of good will and generosity should be able to unite regardless of party or politics . . . we are confronted with a moral issue. It is as old as the scriptures and is as clear as the American Constitution. If an American, because his skin is dark, cannot enjoy the full and free life which all of us want, then who among us would be content to have the colour of his skin changed and stand in his place?

Who among us would then be content with the counsels of patience and delay? One hundred years of delay have passed since President Lincoln freed the slaves, yet their heirs, their grandsons, are not fully free. They are not yet free from the bonds of injustice. They are not yet freed from social and economic oppression, and this nation, for all its hopes and all its boasts, will not be fully free until all its citizens are free. We preach freedom round the world, and we mean it, and we cherish our freedom here at home, but are we to say to the world and, much more importantly, to each other that this is a land of the free except for the Negroes; that we have no second-class citizens except Negroes; that we have no class or caste system, no ghettoes, no master race except with respect to Negroes?

Now the time has come for this nation to fulfil its promises . . . We face a moral crisis as a country and as a people . . . It is not enough to pin the blame on others, to say this is a problem of one section of the country or another, or deplore it. The fact that we face a great change is at hand, and our task, our obligation, is to make that revolution, that change, peaceful and constructive for all.

President Kennedy: *Address to the American people made at The White House on June 11th, 1963*

It is by the finest tints and most insensible gradations that Nature descends from the fairest face about St. James's to the sootiest complexion in Africa. At which tint of these is it, that the ties of blood are to cease? And how many shades must we descend lower still in the scale, ere mercy is to vanish with them?

Laurence Sterne

Look now at warring Christendom. What smallest drop of pity towards sinners is to be found in it? Or how could a spirit all-hellish more fully contrive and hasten their destruction? . . . Again, would you further see the fall of the universal Church from being led by the Spirit of Christ, to be guided by the inspiration of the great fiery dragon, look at all European Christendom sailing round the globe with fire and sword and every murdering art of war to seize the possessions and kill the inhabitants of both the Indies. What natural right of man . . . was not here trodden under foot? . . . And to this day, what wars of Christians against Christians, blended with scalping heathen, still keep staining the earth and the seas with human blood for a miserable share in the spoils of a plundered heathen world? A world which should have heard or seen or felt nothing from the followers of Christ but a divine love that had forced them from distant lands and through the perils of long seas to visit strangers with those glad tidings of peace and salvation to all the world, which angels from Heaven and shepherds on earth proclaimed at the birth of Christ. . . .

It is my complaint against and charge upon all the nations of Christendom that this necessity of murdering arms is the dragon's monster, that is equally brought forth by all and every part of fallen Christendom, and that therefore all and every part, as well Popish as Protestant, are at one and the same distance from the Spirit of their Lord and Saviour. . . . And when this is the state of the Church, the wisdom of this world (which always loves its own) will be in love with it, will spare no cost to maintain it, will make laws, fight battles in defence of it, and condemn every man as heretical who dares speak a word against this glorious image of a Church which the wisdom of this world has set up.

William Law: *An Address to the Clergy*

My ear is pained,
My soul is sick with ev'ry day's report
Of wrong and outrage with which earth is filled.
There is no flash in man's obdurate heart,
It does not feel for man. The nat'ral bond
Of brotherhood is severed as the flax,
That falls asunder at the touch of fire.
He finds his fellow guilty of a skin
Not coloured like his own, and having pow'r
T'enforce the wrong, for such a worthy cause
Dooms and devotes him as his lawful prey.
Lands intersected by a narrow frith
Abhor each other. Mountains interposed
Make enemies of nations, who had else
Like kindred drops been mingled into one.
Thus man devotes his brother, and destroys;
And worse than all, and most to be deplored,
As human nature's broadest, foulest blot,
Chains him, and tasks him, and exacts his sweat
With stripes, that mercy, with a bleeding heart,
Weeps when she sees inflicted on a beast.

*

Sure there is need of social intercourse,
Benevolence and peace and mutual aid
Between the nations, in a world that seems
To toll the death-bell to its own decease.

Cowper: *The Task*

Any doctrine based on racial or colour prejudice and enforced by the State is an affront to human dignity and "ipso facto" an insult to God Himself. . . Unfortunately it is not the isolated cases of cruelty, of sordid motive or of plain stupidity which make the indictment of the pass laws (in S. Africa) so grave a matter. It is the whole foundation upon which they, like the policy of apartheid itself, rest. For, basically, the underlying assumption of the pass laws is just this—that discrimination is justifiable and even commendable if it ensures the permanent superiority of our race over another. And from this assumption, or perhaps as the origin of it, there flows that other even more deadly thing—the depersonalisation of man. ... Racialism in South Africa is the same as racialism everywhere else, and at every moment in the story of mankind.... In the Gospels, there is a background situation which provides an immediate parallel with that of South Africa. There was a fierce and deep-rooted "racial" struggle there in Israel when Christ walked through the cities and villages preaching. "The Jews have no dealings with the Samaritans" ... A historical and a theological situation had combined to produce such a bitterness between the two sections of society that there was a real apartheid; an absolute division. Christ's answer to this situation was the parable of the Good Samaritan. "And who is my neighbour?" had asked the young lawyer, tempting Him. And he was forced to answer his own question, "I suppose that he who showed mercy ..." "Go, and do thou likewise."

There is nothing in the parable which is even a hint that the racial arrogance of the Jew is to be excused or palliated because of his background or his history. There is nothing in it either to indicate that Christ accepted the "official" excuse of the hierarchy for its attitude towards that intolerable division.... The whole point and purpose of the parable is to show that charity, if it is real, must be prepared to break through convention, to shatter preconceptions, to take by force the citadels of prejudice.

Trevor Huddleston: *Naught for your comfort*

We must learn to love others as ourselves: unless we can do this; we not only doom others but are doomed ourselves. But if we can do this there is no problem of racial or any other kind of prejudice, which need overwhelm our judgement.

If we can but renounce our innate determination to regard ourselves as unique and of supreme importance, with everything else ultimately going to the wall, then we can tackle this. But unless we are capable of this renunciation of self-centredness, then we cannot tackle it at all. Love and humility are the only answer to this problem and they must be calmly and vigorously maintained in the face of prejudice, in the face of indignation; of segregation, of all arguments, all the answers about what is good and what is sound, and what is practical for society and so forth; because these answers and arguments are based ultimately on fear, hatred, insecurity and the threat of being regarded as just like other men. Humility then and acceptance, are part of love: and love alone can pay the price for the abandonment of prejudice . . . the roots of prejudice are not in the actual fact of difference; or in the supposed superiority or inferiority of one race to another; persecution arises not primarily out of bitter situation, not out of frictions of human proximity or distrust, which varies by distance, but simply out of the will of living man to think more highly of himself and less highly of others than he ought to think. The essential feature is the inescapable self-centredness, separateness, and tragic personal pride of each individual one of us; whereby we do not love others as ourselves.

Dr. David Stafford-Clark: *The Psychology of Persecution and Prejudice*

The worst of interfering with the customs of simple people, all for their own good, is that it can end by leaving them bereft of their national will to live. . . . Sir Hubert Murray, Administrator of Australian Papua, wanted to rid his territory of the bane of head-hunting. A lesser man might have thought himself justified in using force to suppress so murderous a habit; but not he. He took the trouble to inquire first what head-hunting really meant to the people. He found that a great structure of sane and beneficent social practices was based upon the cult of skulls, and would collapse if head-hunting were to be summarily abolished. His problem was, therefore, to keep the cult alive while doing away with the customary means of maintaining the supply of skulls. He discovered his solution in the fact that pigs, for a number of reasons, enjoyed among the Papuans a personal importance almost equal to that of human beings. Starting from that point, he set out to persuade the folk who lived nearest his capital to adopt pigs' heads instead of human heads for their skull-rituals. He succeeded. The new practice spread to neighbouring districts. There is today a large area of Australian Papua where human head-hunting has been eliminated not only without the use of force but also without damage to the delicately poised social fabric of which it was once the main foundation.

Arthur Grimble: *A Pattern of Islands*

One day I received a letter from the Bihar Government to the following effect: "Your inquiry has been sufficiently prolonged; should you not now bring it to an end and leave Bihar?" The letter was couched in polite language, but its meaning was obvious.

I wrote in reply that the inquiry was bound to be prolonged, and unless and until it resulted in bringing relief to the people, I had no intention of leaving Bihar. I pointed out that it was open to Government to terminate my inquiry by accepting the ryots' grievances as genuine and redressing them, or by recognising that the ryots had made out a prima facie case for an official inquiry which should be immediately instituted.

Sir Edward Gait, the Lieutenant Governor, asked me to see him, expressed his willingness to appoint an inquiry and invited me to be a member of the Committee. . . . I agreed, on condition that I should be free to confer with my co-workers during the progress of the inquiry, that the Government should recognise that, by being a member of the Committee, I did not cease to be the ryots' advocate, and that in case the result of the inquiry failed to give me satisfaction, I should be free to guide and advise the ryots as to what line of action they should take.

Sir Edward Gait accepted the condition as just and proper. . . .

The Committee found in favour of the ryots and recommended that the planters should refund a portion of the exactions made by them which the Committee had found to be unlawful, and that the tinkathia system should be abolished by law. Sir Edward Gait had a large share in getting the agrarian bill passed in accordance with the Committee's recommendations. . . . The planters wielded extraordinary power. They offered strenuous opposition to the bill in spite of the report but Sir Edward Gait remained firm up to the last and fully carried out the recommendations of the Committee. . . .

The ryots, who had all along remained crushed, now somewhat came to their own.

Gandhi: *An Autobiography*

The Viceroy of India at the time of the Mutiny was given the name of Clemency Canning in contemptuous anger. In the face of fierce hostility he insisted on a just and humane policy towards the natives. Demands for indiscriminate vengeance were met with a cool decision. "As long as I have breath in my body I will pursue no other policy . . . I will *not* govern in anger."

His nickname was coined from the resolution of 1859 in which he recommended clemency towards the members of mutinous regiments who yet had not been individually convicted of crime against person or property.

Instead of giving way to racial discrimination Canning did all he could to encourage and create opportunities for educated Indians to acquire responsibility and influence.

Compiled from *Clemency Canning* by Michael Maclagan, and *Two Noble Lives* by Augustus Hall

Hath not a Jew eyes? Hath not a Jew hands, organs, dimensions, senses, affections, passions? fed with the same food, hurt with the same weapons, subject to the same diseases, healed by the same means, warmed and cooled by the same winter and summer, as a Christian is? If you prick us, do we not bleed? If you tickle us, do we not laugh? If you poison us, do we not die?

Shakespeare: *Merchant of Venice*

The outrage of Treblinka and Auschwitz could not have taken place had there not been tens of thousands of men who had grown accustomed to looking at other men as though they were not human at all.

Abba Eban

Cromwell and the Jews

When Cromwell tells Cardinal Mazarin how carefully he must move in this matter, how many Catholics he has "plucked from the fire", and how greatly he hopes to be of use to them in the future, we can believe him in spite of what we know about his obscurantisms and severities on various occasions. He was in many respects more tolerant in fact than was consistent with the views and theories he held.

In this atmosphere a small number of people demanded that toleration should be extended even to non-Christians. In 1649 there had been an appeal from Amsterdam for the readmission of the Jews. . . . When a formal appeal on behalf of that people was made to the Council in England in November 1655 Cromwell appointed a committee to discuss the question and ordered that theological and commercial advice should be taken. Some of the divines proved to be too hostile to the Jewish religion . . . For obvious commercial reasons the merchants were violently opposed to any readmission of the Jews. Cromwell became impatient and decided to settle the matter by administrative action. . . . It was learned from two of the judges that in fact there was nothing in the statute book to prevent the Jews from living in England. The legal resettlement dates from this extra-judicial opinion, which provided an opening for action by Cromwell himself. He adopted a tolerant attitude to the Jews who were already living in the country. He gave private assurances that the recusancy laws would not be put into operation against them . . . These people were soon in possession of their own synagogue and their own cemetery. There was no large-scale readmission, but the numbers gradually grew in the later years of the Protectorate. The whole procedure was typically English; and it is with some justice that the opening of the doors is customarily dated back to the year 1656.

Herbert Butterfield: *Historical Development of the Principle of Toleration in British Life*

Wed. Dec. 12th, 1655. The re-admission of Jews into England

This day "in a withdrawing room at Whitehall, presided over by His Highness, who is much interested in the matter, was held a Conference concerning the Jews", . . . concerning the proposal of admitting Jews, with certain privileges as of alien-citizens, to reside in England. They were banished near 400 years ago: shall they now be allowed to reside and trade again? The Proposer is Manassah Ben Israel, a learned Portuguese Jew of Amsterdam; who, being stirred up of late years by the great things doing in England has petitioned one and the other, Long Parliament and Little Parliament, for this object; but could never till His Highness came into power, get the matter through to a hearing . . . and His Highness spake—and says one witness "I never heard man speak so well". His Highness was eager for the scheme, if so might be. [But it was then decided that] the Jews could not settle here except by private sufferance of His Highness.

Carlyle: *Letters & Speeches of Oliver Cromwell*

For my part I would rather see Ireland totally separated from the Crown of England than kept in obedience only by force. I know of no way of governing mankind but by conciliating them; and according to the forcible way which the Irish have of expressing their meaning, I know of no mode of governing the people, but by letting them have their own way. And what shall we lose by it? If Ireland is governed by conceding to all her ways and wishes, will she be less useful to Great Britain? What is she now? Little more than a diversion for an enemy.

Charles James Fox: *Speeches*

Before allowing its government to involve it in another repetition of the attempt to maintain English dominion over Ireland by brute force, the English nation ought to commune with its conscience, and solemnly reconsider its position ... if the Irish are incapable of being taught the superiority of English notions about the way in which they ought to be governed, and obstinately persist in preferring their own; if this supposition, whichever way we choose to turn it, is true, are we the power which, according to the general fitness of things and the rules of mortality, ought to govern Ireland? If so, what are we dreaming of, when we give our sympathy to the Poles, the Italians, the Hungarians, the Servians, the Greeks, and I know not how many other oppressed nationalities?

J. S. Mill: *England and Ireland 1868*

This land (Sicily) is like one of the many beautiful little girls who are to be seen in the alleys of its townships. The beauty is there in her face beneath the scabs, the dishevelled hair and the torn and tattered clothes; and one can visualise already the look of intelligence and lively nobility which a proper upbringing would give to those features, just as one can imagine the close regard of suffering and near-wickedness which less happy circumstances might breed in its place.

As often happens in under-developed areas, many of the people, intelligent and willing though they be, are imprisoned by their own static world and have not the technical means, nor the education, nor the organising ability to know what to do or how to set to work to improve their conditions. In the face of this impotence, in the land, and in life itself, there remains nothing but sadness and chaos. Some of these people escape. Many are blind to the full extent of their plight, while others understand but give up easily before the massive difficulties with which they are faced and the dangerous hostility of the powerful. Still others have given warning of this waste, and of its enormous scale, insisting that the only way to obtain any concrete, sustained action to eliminate it is for both people and the authorities to meet together to face this and other well-defined problems.

Danilo Dolci: *Waste* (trans. R. Munroe)

In a time of sickness with the pleurisy, a little upward of two years and a half ago, I was brought so near the gates of death, that I forgot my name. Being then desirous to know who I was, I saw a mass of matter of a dull gloomy colour, between the south and the east, and was informed that this mass was human beings in as great misery as they could be, and live, and that I was mixed in with them, and henceforth I might not consider myself as a distinct or separate being. . . . I was then carried in spirit to the mines, where poor oppressed people were digging rich treasures for those called Christians, and heard them blaspheme the name of Christ; at which I was grieved; for his name to me was precious. Then I was informed that these heathen were told that those who oppressed them were the followers of Christ; and they said amongst themselves: "If Christ directed them to use us in this sort, then Christ is a cruel tyrant."

John Woolman: *Journal*

Poor naked wretches, wheresoe'er you are
That bide the pelting of this pitiless storm,
How shall your houseless heads and unfed sides,
Your loop'd and window'd raggedness, defend you
From seasons such as these? . . . Take physic, pomp;
Expose thyself to feel what wretches feel;
That thou may'st shake the superflux to them,
And show the heav'ns more just.

Shakespeare: *King Lear*

The man who desired eternal life was told to sell his goods and give to the poor; and the disciples—to their astonishment—were told that it was easier for a camel to go through a needle's eye than for a rich man to enter into the Kingdom of God. It was but one of many such emphatic and uncompromising sayings in which Jesus condemned wealth. But Jesus did not suggest that the great possessions which deprived the poor of their needs, and the owner of spiritual peace, should be forcibly taken from him, nor did he condemn the man himself. He pitied him for what he was losing spiritually as much as he felt for the sufferings of the poor. Quite the most interesting words in this classic condemnation of wealth are those which Mark records: "Then Jesus, beholding him, loved him". The hard request and the solemn words on the evils of riches did not in the least alter the sympathy and affection with which the man himself was regarded. We do not know the rest of the story, but surely that man, who "went away sorrowful", was given something very serious to consider which no political denunciation could have achieved.

Who knows what seed was sown at that encounter?

Reginald Reynolds: *The Wisdom of John Woolman*

He who toils one year after another to furnish others with wealth and superfluities—who labours and thinks, and thinks and labours, until by overmuch labour he is wearied and oppressed—such a one understands the meaning of that language, "Ye know the Heart of a Stranger, seeing ye were strangers in the land of Egypt". As many at this day, who know not the heart of a stranger, indulge themselves in ways of life which occasion more labour in the world than infinite goodness intends for man, and yet are compassionate toward such in distress who come directly under their observation; were those to change circumstances awhile with some who labour for them; were they to pass regularly through the means of knowing the heart of a stranger, and come to a feeling knowledge of the straits and hardships which many poor innocent people pass through in a hidden obscure life; were these, who now fare sumptuously every day, to act the other part of the scene, till seven times had passed over them, and return again to their former estate; I believe many of them would embrace a way of life less expensive and lighten the heavy burdens of some who now labour out of their sight to support them, and pass through straits with which they are but little acquainted.

John Woolman: *A Plea for the Poor*

Wheel without wheel,
To perplex youth in their outgoings and to bind to labours in Albion
Of day and night the myriads of eternity: that they may grind
And polish brass and iron hour after hour, laborious task,
Kept ignorant of its use: that they might spend the days of wisdom
In sorrowful drudgery to obtain a scanty pittance of bread.

William Blake: *Prophetic Books*

Merely to take one side or other [in a labour dispute] according as the general habit of our mind or the custom of our friends may suggest, is to shirk responsibility. We are not called upon to decide who is right or who is wrong; our duty is something much less habitual—our duty is to think.

And above all our duty is to think out the relation of our religious belief to such occurrences as this. And that relation is singularly close. St. Paul is quite clear that strife, jealousies, wraths, factions, divisions, are the works of the flesh, of that part of our nature which resists the Holy Spirit, whereas the fruits of the Spirit are love and joy and peace. If this is true, the only real solution for our social and industrial chaos is to be found in the power of God's Holy Spirit. But that is the last source to which most of us would apply for guidance. . . . What we call the social problem . . . exists really because people generally are as good as we are and no better. . . . No one ever deliberately planned the state of society which now exists. . . . It is the working out of just our own character—our own selfishness and contempt for humility, our own un-Christ-likeness.

William Temple: *Sermons*

Edmund Burke's tribute to John Howard, 1780

I cannot name this gentleman without remarking that his labours and writings have done much to open the eyes and hearts of mankind. He has visited all Europe—not to survey the sumptuousness of palaces, or the stateliness of temples; not to make accurate measurements of the remains of ancient grandeur, nor to form a scale of the curiosity of modern art; not to collect medals or collate manuscripts—but to dive into the depths of dungeons and plunge into the infection of hospitals; to survey the mansions of sorrow and pain; to take the gauge and measure of misery, depression and contempt; to remember the forgotten, to attend to the neglected, to visit the forsaken, and compare and collate the miseries of all men in all countries. His plan is original and it is full of genius as it is of humanity.

Edmund Burke: *Speeches*

Those gentlemen who, when they are told of the misery our prisoners suffer, content themselves with saying, let them keep out, prefaced perhaps with an angry prayer, seem not duly sensible of the favour of Providence which distinguishes them from the sufferers: they do not remember that we are required to imitate our gracious Heavenly Parent, who is kind to the unthankful and to the evil: they also forget the vicissitude of human affairs: the unexpected changes to which all men are liable; and that those whose circumstances are affluent, may in time be reduced to indigence and become debtors and prisoners. And as to criminality, it is possible that a man who has often shuddered at hearing the account of a murder may, on a sudden temptation, commit that very crime. Let him that thinks he standeth take heed lest he fall and commiserate those that are fallen.

To reform prisoners should always be the leading view in every house of correction . . . as rational and immortal beings, we owe this to them; nor can any criminality of things justify our neglect in this particular.

John Howard: *The State of Prisons*

The first prison I ever saw had inscribed on it CEASE TO DO EVIL: LEARN TO DO WELL; but as the inscription was on the outside, the prisoners could not read it. It should have been addressed to the self-righteous free spectator in the street, and should have run ALL HAVE SINNED, AND FALLEN SHORT OF THE GLORY OF GOD.

G. B. Shaw: Preface to *Imprisonment* (*English Local Government*) by Sidney and Beatrice Webb

[Elizabeth Fry, after setting on foot reforms in the English prisons, toured the continent on a mission of mercy. Her firm but gentle and persuasive methods were often most successful, as here, at Hanover.]

I found there more than a thousand prisoners (mostly confined for small crimes) loaded with heavy chains. I was so touched by their misery that it tempted me to represent the cruelty and injustice of their treatment to the Government. A few weeks after, when I visited the prison again, I found, to my surprise and pleasure, that my remonstrance had been listened to, and the chains taken off all the prisoners. . . . When I visited the prison the second time, I could not help being rather amused, though at the same time grieved, when I remarked a number of little leaden images of the Virgin. Mentioning that they were not there when I was there before, I was told that, after my departure, the prisoners had been so impressed by the importance of religion that they had each bought a Virgin!

Elizabeth Fry: *Journal*

It is very hard to convince the ordinary citizen that the criminal is not better off than he deserves to be, and indeed on the verge of being positively pampered. Judges, magistrates, and Home Secretaries are so commonly under the same delusion that people who have ascertained the truth about prisons have been driven to declare that the most urgent necessity of the situation is that every judge, magistrate, and Home Secretary should serve a six months sentence incognito; so that when he is dealing out and enforcing sentences he should at least know what he is doing . . . the official reports tell us only of the care that is taken of the prisoner and the advantages he enjoys, or can earn by good conduct, never of his sufferings; and the public is not imaginative or thoughtful enough to supply the deficiency.

G. B. Shaw. Preface to *Imprisonment* (*English Local Government*) by Sidney and Beatrice Webb

Charles James Fox has been described as "the first great English Statesmen whose reverence for toleration was absolute". At the time of the Gordon riots he defended the Catholics. "He could not think the papist religion incompatible with government nor civil liberty; because in looking round the world he saw that in Switzerland, where democracy reigned universally in the fullest measure, it flourished most in cantons professing that religion."

Unitarians were as unpopular as Catholics, and even the tolerant Locke wrote that "they were not to be tolerated".

Fox, only, spoke up for them. "Dr. South, in speaking of them, has traced their pedigree from wretch to wretch back to the devil himself. These descendants of the devil are my clients."

Compiled from *Charles James Fox*. J. L. and B. Hammond

I hope in this condemnation of the Catholic religion in which I sincerely join their worst Enemies, I shall not be so far mistaken as to have it supposed that I would convey the slightest approbation of any Laws which disqualify and incapacitate any class of men for Civil offices on account of religious opinions. I consider all such Laws as fatal, and lamentable mistakes in Legislation. They are the mistakes of troubled times, and half barbarous ages. All Europe is gradually emerging from their influence. This Country has lately made a noble and successful Effort for their abolition. In proportion as this Example is followed I firmly believe the Enemies of Church and state will be lessened and the foundations of peace, order and happiness will receive additional Strength. I cannot discuss the uses and abuses of this day without touching upon the errors of the Catholic faith from which we have escaped; but I should be beyond measure concerned if a condemnation of Theological Errors were construed into an approbation of laws so deeply marked by the Spirit of Intolerance—.

Sydney Smith: *Letter to Lady Holland*

The Unitarians think the doctrine of the Trinity to be a profanation of the Scriptures; you compel them to marry in your churches, or rather, I should say, we compel them to marry in our churches; and when the male and female Dissenter are kneeling before the altar, much is said to them by the priest, of this, to them, abhorred doctrine. They are about to petition Parliament that their marriages may be put upon the same footing as those of Catholics and Quakers. The principles of religious liberty which I have learnt (perhaps under you) make me their friend in the question; and if you approve, I will write an article upon it.

Of course Methodists, when attacked, cry out, "Infidel! Atheist!" —these are the weapons with which all fanatics and bigots fight; but should we be intimidated by this, if we do not deserve it? And does it follow that any examination of the faults of Dissenters is a panegyric upon the Church of England? But these are idle questions, as I do not mean to review it. I have written an article upon Dissenters' marriages, which I will send the moment I get some books from town.

Sydney Smith: *Letter to Francis Jeffrey*

What I want to see the State do is to lessen in these sad times some of their numerous enemies. Why not do something for the

Catholics and scratch them off the list? Then comes the Protestant Dissenters. Then of measures,—a mitigation of the game-laws—commutation of tithes—granting to such towns as Birmingham and Manchester the seats in Parliament taken from the rottenness of Cornwall—revision of the Penal Code—sale of the Crown lands—sacrifice of the Droits of Admiralty against a new war;—anything that would show the Government to the people in some other attitude than that of taxing, punishing, and restraining.

Sydney Smith: *Letters*

The sun itself is not more common and open to all than the teaching of Christ. . . . I wish that even the weakest woman should read the Gospels—should read the epistle of Paul. And I wish these were translated into all languages, so that they might be read and understood, not only by Scots and Irishmen, but also by Turks and Saracens. I long that the husbandman should sing portions of them to himself as he follows the plough, that the weaver should hum them to the tune of his shuttle, that the traveller should beguile with their stories the tedium of his journey.

Erasmus: Preface to *Novum Instrumentum*

I have often thought of it as one of the most barbarous customs in the world, considering us as a civilised and a Christian country, that we deny the advantages of learning to a woman. We reproach the sex every day with folly and impertinence, while I am confident, had they the advantages of education equal to us, they would be guilty of less than ourselves . . . it is manifest that as the rational soul distinguishes us from brutes, so education carries on the distinction and makes some less brutish than others. . . . But why then should women be denied the benefit of instruction? . . . The capacities of women are supposed to be greater and their senses quicker than those of the men; and what they might be capable of being bred to is plain for some instances of female wit, which this age is not without; which upbraids us with injustice, and looks as if we denied women the advantages of education for fear they should vie with men in their improvements. To remove this objection, and that women might have at least a needful opportunity of education in all sorts of useful learning, I propose the draught of an academy for that purpose.

Defoe: *An Academy for Women*

I say that both male and female are cast in one same mould; instruction and custom excepted, there is no great difference between them. Plato calleth them both indifferently to the society of all studies, exercises, charges, and functions of war and peace in his commonwealth. And the philosopher Antisthenes took away all distinction between their virtue and ours.

Montaigne (trans. Florio)

[Erasmus defends women in his colloquy between the Abbot and the Learned Woman.]

ANTRONIUS,* THE ABBOT: What sort of Household Stuff do I see?

MAGDALIA: Is it not that which is neat?

ANT: How neat it is, I can't tell, but I am sure it is not very becoming either a Maid or a Matron.

MAG: Why so?

ANT: Because here's Books lying about everywhere.

MAG: What, have you liv'd to this Age, and are both an Abbot and a Courtier, and never saw any Books in a Lady's Apartment?

ANT: Yes, I have seen Books, but they were French; but here I see Greek and Latin ones.

MAG: Why, are there no other Books but French that teach Wisdom?

* The name is derived from the Greek, meaning a big Ass.

ANT: But it becomes Ladies to have something that is diverting, to pass away their leisure Hours.

MAG: Must none but Ladies be wise and live pleasantly?

ANT: You very improperly connect being wise and living pleasantly together; Women have nothing to do with Wisdom.

*

MAG: But why does this Household Stuff displease you?

ANT: Because a Spinning-Wheel is a Woman's Weapon.

MAG: Is it not a Woman's Business to mind the Affairs of her Family and to instruct her Children?

ANT: Yes, it is.

MAG: And do you think so weighty an Office can be executed without Wisdom?

ANT: I believe not.

MAG: This Wisdom I learn from Books.

ANT: I could dispense with Books; but I can't bear Latin books.

MAG: Why so?

ANT: Because that Tongue is not fit for a Woman.

MAG: I want to know the Reason.

*

ANT: The common People are of my Mind, because it is such a rare unusual thing for a Woman to understand Latin.

MAG: What do you tell me of the Common People for, who are the worst examples in the World that can be follow'd? What have I to do with Custom, that is the Mistress of all evil Practices? We ought to accustom ourselves to the best Things:

*

ANT: I have often heard it said, that a wise Woman is twice a Fool.

MAG: That indeed has been often said; but it was by Fools. A Woman that is truly wise does not think her-self so: But on the contrary, one that knows nothing, thinks herself to be wise, and that is being twice a Fool.

ANT: I can't well tell how it is, that as Panniers don't become an Ox, so neither does Learning become a Woman.

*

MAG: Indeed? What did Paula and Eustochium do? Did not they converse with the holy Scriptures?

ANT: Ay, but this is a rare Thing now.

MAG: ... It is not so great a Rarity as you think it. There are both in Spain and Italy not a few Women, that are able to vye with the Men, and there are the More-ites in England, and the Bilibald-duks and Blaureticks in Germany. So that unless you take care of yourselves it will come to pass that we shall be Divinity-Professors in the Schools, and preach in the Churches, and take Possession of your Mitres.

ANT: God forbid.

Erasmus: *Colloquies*

The inequality of rights between men and women has no other source than the law of the strongest. ... Was there ever any domination which did not appear natural to those who possessed it?

... We ought not to ordain that to be born a girl instead of a boy, any more than to be born black instead of white, shall decide the person's position through all life.

... In all things of any difficulty and importance, those who can do them well are fewer than the need, even with the most unrestricted latitude of choice: and any limitation of the field of selection deprives society of some chances of being served by the competent without ever saving it from the incompetent.

If it be said that the doctrine of the equality of the sexes rests only on theory, it must be remembered that the contrary doctrine also has only theory to rest upon... The profoundest knowledge of the laws of the formation of character is indispensable to entitle any one to affirm even that there is any difference, much more what the difference is, between the two sexes considered as moral and rational beings.

J. S. Mill: *The Subjection of Women*

In the person of Womankind

Men, if you love us, play no more
The fools or tyrants with your friends,
To make us still sing o'er and o'er
Our own false praises, for your ends:
We have both wits and fancies too,
And if we must, let's sing of you.
Nor do we doubt but that we can,
If we would search with care and pain
Find some one good in some one man;
So, going through all your strain,
We shall at last of parcels make
One good enough for a song's sake,
And as a cunning painter takes,
In any curious piece you see,
More pleasure while the thing he makes,
Than when 'tis made—why, so will we;
And having pleased our art, we'll try
To make a new, and hang that by.

Ben Jonson

A colloquy between Eutrapelus and Fabiella

Fab. I believe you judge that a Male is naturally more excellent and strong than a Female?

Eu. I believe they are.

Fab. That is Men's Opinion. But are Men any Thing longer-lived than Women? Are they free from Distempers?

Eu. No, but in general they are stronger.

Fab. But then they themselves are excell'd by Camels in Strength.

Eu. But besides, the Male was created first.

Fab. So was Adam before Christ. Artists use to be most exquisite in their later Performances.

Eu. But God put the Woman under Subjection to the Man.

Fab. It does not follow of Consequence, that he is the better because he commands.

EU. . . . [But what did Paul] mean when he wrote to the Corinthians, that "Christ was the Head of the Man, and Man the Head of the Woman"?

FAB. . . . Answer me this Question, Whether or no it is given to Men alone, to be the Members of Christ?

EU. God forbid, that is given to all Men and Women too by Faith.

FAB. How comes it about then, that when there is but one Head, it should not be common to all the Members?

EU. But we Men alone fight for our Country.

FAB. And you Men often desert from your Colours, and run away like Cowards; and it is not always for the Sake of your Country, that you leave your Wives and Children, but for the Sake of a little nasty Pay; . . . and now after all your Boasting of your warlike Prowess, there is none of you all, but if you had once experienced what it is to bring a Child into the World, would rather be placed ten Times in the Front of a Battle, then undergo once what we must so often.

Erasmus: *Colloquies*

One day, when a certain Abbot, much reputed for his piety, spake with Anselm concerning divers points of Monastic Religion, and conversed among other things of the boys that were brought up in the cloister, he added: "What, pray, can we do with them? They are perverse and incorrigible; day and night we cease not to chastise them, yet they grow worse and worse."

Whereat Anselm marvelled, and said, "Ye cease not to beat them? And when they are grown to manhood, of what sort are they then?"

"They are dull and brutish," said the other.

Then said Anselm, "With what good profit do ye expend your substance in nurturing human beings till they become brute beasts? . . . But I prithee tell me, for God's sake, wherefore ye are so set against them? Are they not human, sharing in the same nature as yourselves? Would ye wish to be so handled as ye handle them?"

G. G. Coulton: *Medieval Garner*

(Children) are Travellers newly arrived in a strange Country, of which they know nothing. . . . And though their Questions seem sometimes not very material, yet they should be seriously answered.

If you or I now should be set down in Japan, . . . we should no doubt . . . ask a Thousand Questions, which to a supercilious or inconsiderate Japaner, would seem very idle and impertinent; though to us they would be very material . . . and we should be glad to find a Man so complaisant and courteous, as to satisfie our Demands, and instruct our Ignorance.

Locke: *On Education*

It is desirable that instruction should not be forced on children. We should never coax children; if we do, we teach them to disguise the truth, and they never forget it. We must lead them by reason as much as possible. . . . The pleasure we derive from playful children often spoils them . . . Let us mingle instruction with their plays, let Wisdom show herself but at intervals and with a smiling face . . . Do not be astonished at their failings; but on the contrary pity their weaknesses.

We must always begin with open, gay and friendly behaviour without trifling. We must often tolerate things which we wish to correct and wait for the moment when the mind of the child will be in a state to profit by instruction . . . We have no right to require from them more than they can give. When we speak to them of words and things that they do not understand, we often leave a dangerous impression of ennui and sadness on their minds. Of all the faculties of children reason is the only one on which we can depend; if we cultivate it carefully it always grows with them.

Fénelon: *On the Education of Girls*

I cannot but often wonder to see Fathers, who love their Sons very well, yet order the matter by a constant Stiffness, and a mien of Authority and distance to them all their Lives, as if they were never to enjoy, or have any comfort from those they love best in the World. . . .

The Reservedness and Distance, that Fathers often keep, often deprive their Sons of that refuge, which would be of more Advantage to them, than an hundred Rebukes and Chidings. . . . Would you have him open his Heart to you, and ask your Advice? You must begin to do so with him first. . . . But whatever he consults you about, unless it lead to some fatal and irremediable Mischief, be sure you advise one as a Friend of more Experience; but with your Advice mingle nothing of Command or Authority, not more than you would to your Equal or a Stranger. . . . You must consider that he is a Young Man, and has Pleasures and Fancies, which you are pass'd. You must not expect his Inclinations should be just as yours, nor that at Twenty he should have the same Thoughts as you have at Fifty. . . . Ask *his* Advice; and when he ever lights on the Right, follow it as his; and if it succeeds well, let him have the Commendation.

Locke: *On Education*

Is this a holy thing to see
In a rich and fruitful land,
Babes reduced to misery,
Fed with cold and usurous hand?

Is that trembling cry a song?
Can it be a song of joy?
And so many children poor?
It is a land of poverty!

And their sun does never shine,
And their fields are bleak and bare,
And their ways are filled with thorns:
It is eternal winter there.

Blake: *Songs of Experience*

Lord Shaftesbury was, in spite of a narrow-minded theological intolerance, full of a wide sympathy for all the exploited poor, especially for children. J. L. and B. Hammond in their *Life* say of him, "His intolerance was of the head and not the heart. If you watched the play of his compassion, you would conclude that he was as liberal-minded a man as Gladstone or Huxley or Mill." He never gave up. In 1854 his Bill to prohibit the use of chimney climbing boys under the age of sixteen was rejected "as a pitiful cant of pseudo philanthropy", "without a word of sympathy for the wretched children". In 1872 Shaftesbury tried again. "Years of oppression and cruelty have rolled on, and now death [of a boy] has given me the power of one more appeal through the *Times*." Again there was little support for him. In 1875 he again brought this evil before the public without success. It was not till 1878 that he could write in his Diary, "Was much disheartened at outset, House very inattentive—had twice to implore their condescension to hear me. At last they listened and, so far as their understanding natures would allow, applauded me. The *Times*, may the paper be blessed, has assisted me gloriously."

Compiled from *Lord Shaftesbury*. J. L. and B. Hammond

Charles Booth, 1840–1916, carried on (entirely at his own expense) over a period of seventeen years a patient investigation of how the poor of London lived and worked. The condition of the child was perhaps the saddest feature in Charles Booth's picture: "Puny, pale-faced, scantily clad and badly shod, these small and feeble folk may be found sitting limp and chill on the school benches in all the poorer parts of London. They swell the bills of mortality as want and sickness thin them off, or survive to be the needy and enfeebled adults whose burden of helplessness the next generation will have to bear."

Beatrice Webb: *My Apprenticeship*

[Don Mario Borelli, an Italian priest, pleads with his superior the Archbishop of Naples for permission to work among "the scugnizzi", the outcast children of the city.]

"Your Excellency, you must understand something of what the life of the streets does to these children. You must know that to be a scugnizzo is to have a man's soul in the body of a child. It is to have suffered in that body the rape of innocence, the pain of hunger, the bleak, desert cold of the city. To be a scugnizzo is to live without love, to trust no one, because the one you trust will snatch the bread from your mouth or the cigarettes from your pocket. To be a scugnizzo is to know that every woman is a whore, and every man is a thief, that every policeman is a sadist and every priest a liar. If I went among them as I am now, they would laugh at me or spit in my face. If I offered them a home they would tell me that the carabinieri offer them a home, too—in a house of correction. I should never come within a hand's reach of them. Believe me, Your Excellency . . . Believe me! I was born in the bassi. I know!"

[Permission was granted to him, and for over ten years now he has devoted himself to the outcasts of Naples. He lived at first among them as one of them and then, having gradually gained their confidence, gave them shelter, food, security, education, love. In pleading for help to carry on his work he reminds us that friendless children are the responsibility of all.]

"That is the thing to understand. We are all one family, all of us! We are sons and daughters of one Father—Arabs, Greeks, Indians, Chinese, even Neapolitans! If one of us is ill, the infection touches all the rest. An injustice done to one is an injustice to the whole family . . . [All] are committed now, as part of this human family. They are committed to its future as to its present."

Morris West: *Children of the Sun*

II

Charity towards individuals—between states, races, nationalities and creeds

But, Lord, amende us alle
And give us grace, good God, Charite to folwe.

Langland

If this Notion be not understood and admitted; that Difference of Opinion in some matters about Religion, shou'd not make difference in Affection; we shall all be the worse for our Religion.

Benjamin Whichcote

Even in the face of annihilation, the obliterator of all distinctions, we cannot help clinging to the most arbitrary one of the "we" and "they". How can we acquire, before it is too late, the instinctive habit of always and radically thinking in terms of "we"?

Werner Pelz

Religion is *not* a Hear-say, a Presumption, a Supposition; is not a customary Pretension and Profession; is not an Affectation of any Mode; is not a Piety of particular Fancy, consisting in some pathetic Devotions, vehement Expressions, bodily Severities, affected Anomalies and Aversions from the innocent Usages of others; but consisteth in a profound Humility, and an universal Charity.

Nathaniel Culverwel

I speak now not to men but to Thee, O God of all beings, all worlds and all ages. If weak creatures, lost in infinity, may dare to ask something of Thee, the giver of all things, whose decrees are as immutable as they are eternal, then deign to look mercifully upon the faults which are inseparable from our nature; let them not destroy us.

Thou didst not give us hearts for hating one another, nor countries for butchering one another; grant that we may rather help each other to bear the burden of an arduous and transitory life; may the trifling differences between the clothes which cover our puny bodies, between all our inadequate languages, all our absurd customs, all our imperfect laws, all our circumstances, so varied in our own eyes yet so much the same to Thee—may all these differences, which distinguish the atoms known as man, not engender hatred and persecution. May those who light candles in Thy honour suffer those who are content with the light of Thy sun. May there be no hatred between those who cover their robes with white linen vestments to bid us love Thee and those who command the same in black woollen gown. Let it be indifferent whether we worship Thee in a bastard form of an ancient tongue or in a newer jargon. May those whose vesture is dyed red or purple, who lord it over a small plot of this little mud-heap, the earth, and possess some few roundels of one particular metal enjoy without arrogant superiority their supposed greatness and wealth which others regard without envious emulation; for Thou knowest that in these varieties there is nothing for envy or pride.

May all men remember that they are brothers! May they abhor all tyranny over the human spirit even as now they abominate the brigandage which seizes by force the fruits of toil and peaceful industry! If wars there must be, at least let us not hate each other, and in the unity of peace let us not turn and rend each other; rather let us employ our moment of life to join, from Siam to California, our thousand varying tongues to bless Thy goodness in bestowing this moment upon us.

Voltaire: *Traité de la Tolérance, 1763*

COUNTESS And the good soldiers, Bella, take care of them.
They're being put to so much trouble.
BELLA Who started it, madam?
COUNTESS A lot of time would be wasted
Going back through the years to answer that.
We could scarcely be of our own time if we would,
Being moved about by such very old disturbances.
If we could wake each morning with no memory
Of living before we went to sleep, we might
Arrive at a faultless day, once in a great many,
But the hardest frost of a year
Will not arrest the growing world
As blame and the memory of wrong will do.
JANET Then you have no thought for the downtrodden men,
The overlong injustice, madam?
COUNTESS Not
As they are downtrodden, but as they are men
I think of them, as they should think of those
Who oppress them. We gain so little by the change
When the downtrodden in their turn tread down.
But then, deserters all, we should all change sides,
I dare say; and that would be proper behaviour
For a changeable world, and no more tiring
Than to go to the extraordinary lengths
Which men will go to, to be identical
Each day.

Christopher Fry: *The Dark is Light Enough*

With everything, whether it is above or below, remote or near, visible or invisible, thou shalt preserve a relation of unlimited love without any animosity or without a desire to kill. To live in such a consciousness while standing or walking, sitting or lying down till you are asleep, is Brahma vihara, or, in other words, is living and moving and having your joy in the spirit of Brahma.

The Buddha

If anyone can convince and show me that some view or action of mine is wrong, I will cheerfully change; I seek the truth which never yet hurt any man. . . .

Does the sun claim the rain's work? or Æsculapius that of Ceres? or take each single star—are not all different yet all co-operating to the same end? . . .

Here one thing is of real worth, to live out life in truth and justice, with charity even to the false and unjust. . . .

Remember that to change your course and to accept correction is no surrender of freedom. Your action follows your own impulse and judgement, and keeps the course which your own mind sets. If the fault rests with you, why do it? if with another, with what do you find fault? the atoms or the gods? Either is idiocy. *Find fault with nobody*. If you can, set the doer right; if that is impossible, at least set the thing right; if even that cannot be, to what purpose is your fault-finding?

Marcus Aurelius

As in the Arke there were Lions, but the Lion shut his mouth, and clincht his paw, (the Lion hurt nothing in the Arke), and in the Arke there were Vipers and Scorpions, but the Viper shewed no teeth, nor the Scorpion no taile, (the Viper bit none, the Scorpion stung none in the Arke) (for, if they had occasioned any disorder there, their escape could have been but into the Sea, into irreparable ruine) so, in every State, (though that State be an Arke of peace, and preservation) there will be some kind of oppression in some Lions, some that will abuse their power; but Vae si scandalizemur, woe unto us if we be scandalized with that . . . It is the chafing of the Lion and the stirring of the Viper, that aggravates the danger; . . . He is a good Christian that can ride out, or board out, or hull out a storme, that by industry, as long as he can, and by patience, when he can do no more, over-lives a storm, and does not forsake his ship for it, that is not scandalized with that State, nor that Church, of which he is a member, for those abuses that are in it. The Arke is peace, peace is good dispositions to one another, good interpretations of one another; for, if our impatience put us from our peace, and so out of the Arke, all without the Arke is sea;

John Donne: *Sermons*

Then gently scan your brother man,
Still gentler, sister woman;
Though they may gang a kennin' wrang,
To step aside is human:
One point must still be greatly dark,
The moving *Why* they do it;
And just as lamely can ye mark
How far, perhaps, they rue it.

Who made the heart, 'tis He alone
Decidedly can try us;
He knows each chord—its various tone,
Each spring—its various bias:
Then at the balance let's be mute,
We never can adjust it;
What's done we partly may compute,
But know not what's resisted.

Robert Burns

No man can justly censure or condemn another, because indeed no man truly knows another. This I perceive in myself; for I am in the dark to all the world, and my nearest friends behold me but in a cloud: those that know me but superficially, think less of me than I do of myself; those of my near acquaintance think more. God, who truly knows me, knows that I am nothing; for he only beholds me, and all the world; who looks not on us through a derived ray, or a trajection of a sensible species, but beholds the substance without the helps of accidents, and the forms of things, as we their operations. Further no man can judge another, because no man knows himself; for we censure others but as they disagree from that humour which we fancy laudable in ourselves, and commend others but for that wherein they seem to quadrate and consent with us. So that in conclusion, all is but that we all condemn, self-love.

Sir Thomas Browne: *Religio Medici*

In judging others we can see too well
Their grievous fall, but not how grieved they fell;
Judging ourselves, we to our minds recall
Not how we fell, but how we grieved to fall.

Crabbe

It is not the best who are found to be the severest censors and judges of others. Quickness to detect and expose the weakness of a fellow man . . . are not the characteristics which experience would lead us to expect in a noble nature . . . and it is not seldom the men and women whose own moral nature is weak, who are the least forbearing. . . . Whether it be that the secret sense of insecure virtue seeks re-assurance by assuming infallibility . . . or that unconsciously we try to indemnify conscience for our own defects . . . by taking a tone of moral indignation . . . rigidity and sternness is often the signs of a nature that greatly needs indulgence for its own defects. On the other hand to be forbearing . . . to be averse to see or hear of human faults . . . to be considerate of every extenuating circumstance (does not this) betoken, not moral apathy or indifference, but the nature which is beyond all personal sympathy with vice? And if thus, human goodness is the more merciful in proportion as it approaches nearer to perfection, if amongst men the highest spirituality is the most tolerant . . . might we not conclude that when goodness becomes absolutely perfect, just then will mercy become absolutely unlimited?

John Caird: *University Sermons*

Hee reckons more inconveniencys then you doe that ffollow good natur's, say's it makes one credulous, apt to bee abused, betrays one to the cunning of People that make advantage on't and a thousand such things, which I hear half asleep and halfe awake and take litle notice of, unlesse it bee somtimes to say that with all these faults I would not bee without it, noe, in Earnest, nor I could not love any Person that I thought had it not to a good degree, twas the first thing I liked in you, and without it I should nere have liked any thing; I know tis counted simple but I cannot imagin why, tis true some People have it that have not witt but there are at least as many foolish People that have noe good Nature, and those are the person's I have ever observed to bee fullest of tricks, litle ugly plotts, and design's, unnecessary disguise, and mean Cunnings . . . some will say they are cunning only in theire owne defence and that there is noe liveing in this world without it, but I cannot understand how any thing more is necessary to on's owne safety besides a prudent caution . . . I remember my Mother [said] "I have lived to see that tis almost impossible to think People worse than they are, and soe will you". I did not beleeve her.

Dorothy Osborne: *Letters to Sir William Temple*

Man is not made for justice from his fellow, but for love which is greater than justice, and by including supersedes justice. *Mere* justice is an impossibility, a fiction of analysis . . . Love is the law of our condition, without which we can no more render justice than a man can keep a straight line, walking in the dark.

George Macdonald: *Love Thine Enemy*

That conversion will always be suspected that apparently concurs with interest. He that never finds his error till it hinders his progress towards wealth or honour will not be thought to love Truth only for herself. Yet it may easily happen that information may come at a commodious time, and as truth and interest are not by any fatal necessity at variance, that one may by accident introduce the other. . . . It is natural to hope that a comprehensive is likewise an elevated soul, and that whoever is wise is also honest. I am willing to believe that Dryden, having employed his mind, active as it was, upon different studies, and filled it, capacious as it was, with other materials, came unprovided to the controversy, and wanted rather skill to discover the right than virtue to maintain it. But enquiries into the heart are not for man; we must now leave him to his Judge.

Dr. Johnson on Dryden: *Lives of the Poets*

Aba Agathon used to say to himself, whensoever he saw any act or anything which his thought wished to judge or condemn, "Do not commit the thing thyself", and in this manner he quieted his mind, and held his peace.

The Paradise of the Fathers

A Brother asked an old man, saying, "How shall I be able to avoid despising my brother?" The old man said unto him, "We and our neighbour are two faces. Now if we provide the mirror of prayer we shall see the beam in our own eye, and we shall also see in the mirror the face of our brother polished and pure."

The Paradise of the Fathers

We fancy that our patience could endure great strain and trial, while we give way to impatience under very trifling provocations: we think we could nurse a neighbour in grievous sickness, but we cannot put up with his ill-temper, his awkwardness or incivility, above all with his importunity when he worries us in season and out of season with talk about matters which we count as absurd or trivial. Then we make excuses for our impatience on the ground of loss of time . . . forgetting that we spend time in many a pursuit which is more unprofitable than forbearance towards a neighbour . . . at the worst one must deal with a troublesome neighbour as children swallow physic, with our eyes shut.

Jean Pierre Camus: *The Spirit of S. Francis de Sales* (trans. H. L. Sidney Lear)

The Master said, "In serving his father and mother a man may gently remonstrate with them. But if he sees that he has failed to change their opinion, he should resume an attitude of deference and not thwart them; (he) may feel discouraged, but not resentful."

The Analects of Confucius (trans. Arthur Waley)

Tzu-Kung was always criticizing other people. The Master said, "It is fortunate for Tzu that he is so perfect himself as to have time to spare for this. I myself have none."

The Analects of Confucius (trans. Arthur Waley)

Our souls may lose their peace and even disturb other people's if we are always criticising trivial actions which often are not real defects at all, but we construe them wrongly through ignorance of their motives.

St. Teresa: *The Interior Castle*

Neither can I be angry with my brother, or quarrel with him; for we are made for co-operation, like the feet, the hands, the eyelids, the upper and lower rows of teeth. To thwart one another is contrary to nature; and one form of thwarting is resentment and estrangement. . . .

When offended at a fault in someone else divert your thoughts to the reflection, What is the parallel fault in me? Is it attachment to money? or pleasure? or reputation? as the case may be. Dwelling on this, anger forgets itself and makes way for the thought—"He cannot help himself—what else can he do?" If it is not so, enable him, if you can to help himself.

Marcus Aurelius

[Sir Walter Scott was a man of such sincere humility that we can believe him when he said to his friend, Mr. Skene:]

And God knows, if I have enemies, this I may at least with truth say, that I have never wittingly given cause of enmity in the whole course of my life, for even the burnings of political hate seemed to find nothing in my nature to feed the flame. I am not conscious of having borne a grudge towards any man, and at this moment of my overthrow, so help me God, I wish well and feel kindly to everyone. And if I thought that any of my works contained a sentence hurtful to anyone's feelings, I would burn it. I think even my novels are free from that blame.

Sir Walter Scott: *Journal*

I have written against —— one of the cleverest pamphlets I ever read, which I think would cover —— and him with ridicule. At least it made me laugh very much in reading it; and there I stood, with the printer's devil, and the real devil close to me; and then I said, "After all, this is very funny, and very well written, but it will give great pain to people who have been very kind and good to me through life; and what can I do to show my sense of that kindness, if it is not by flinging this pamphlet into the fire?" So I flung it in, and there was an end!

Sydney Smith: *Letter to Lady Holland*

You will smile when I tell you I think myself the only woman in the world who could live with a brother's wife and make a real friend of her, . . . partly from a knack I know I have of looking into people's real characters and never expecting them to act out of it—never expecting another to do as I would in the same case. When you leave your mother, and say, if you never shall see her again, you shall feel no remorse; and when you make a Jewish bargain with your Lover; all this gives me no offence, because it is your nature, and your temper, and I do not expect or want you to be otherwise than you are. I love you for the good that is in you, and look for no change.

Mary Lamb to Sarah Stoddart

The want of love we can only acknowledge in the power of love. And it seems to me that the refusal to believe ourselves in God's love and to tell others of it by our lips and our lives is the great sin of all . . . To go on eating and drinking to the day before the flood is not so bad as to go on railing and disputing, and I am afraid we are guilty of both sins. We are not the less given to self-indulgence, in the ordinary sense, because we find another cheaper luxury in calling names. I would not throw stones, for every one comes back to myself, and I feel truly that there is no bitterness in any one's heart in which I am not a sharer.

F. D. Maurice: *Letters*

Endeavour to be patient in bearing with defects and infirmities in others, of what kind soever; because thou also hast many things which others must bear with. If thou canst not make thyself such as thou wouldst, how canst thou expect to have another according to thy liking? We would fain have others perfect, and yet we amend not our own defects. We would have others strictly corrected, but will not be corrected ourselves. The large liberty of others displeases us, and yet we would not be denied anything we ask for. We wish others to be bound down by laws, and we suffer ourselves to be in no sort restrained. Thus it is clear how seldom we weigh our neighbour as we weigh ourselves. If all were perfect, what then should we have to suffer from others for God's sake? But now God has so ordered it, that we learn to bear one another's burdens; for there is no man without defect, no one without his burden, no man sufficient for himself, no man wise enough for himself; but we must support one another, comfort one another, assist, instruct, and admonish one another.

Thomas à Kempis: *Of the Imitation of Christ*

Fly a thousand leagues away from saying, "I was in the *right*: it was not *right* for me to suffer this, they had no *right* to do such a thing to me." Now God deliver us from such wrong rights! Do you think that there was any question of rights when Jesus suffered the injuries which were so unrighteously inflicted on Him. . . . When we receive honours or affection or kind treatment let us think what right have we to them—for certainly we have no *right* to them in this life.

St. Teresa: *The Way of Perfection*

Francis recommended us to imitate the good Samaritan who poured oil and wine into the wounds he sought to heal. It was a frequent saying of his that it takes more oil than vinegar and salt to make a good salad. Another of his favourite sayings was, "Always be as indulgent as you can, remembering that one can catch more flies with a spoonful of honey than with a hundred barrels of vinegar." . . . "But," I answered, "truth must always be truth, however given or taken;" and I quoted S. Paul's words to Timothy: "Preach the word; be instant in season, out of season, reprove, rebuke, exhort with all long-suffering and doctrine." "Yes," Francis replied, "but the gist of the apostolic precept lies in those two words, long-suffering and doctrine. Doctrine means truth, and truth should be told patiently. I mean we should be prepared to see it rejected. . . . Every man who seeks to lead others in the path of righteousness must make up his mind to bear their inconsistency and injustice . . . truth which is not charitable springs from a charity which is not true."

Jean Pierre Camus: *The Spirit of S. Francis de Sales* (trans. H. L. Sidney Lear)

Nothing softeneth the arrogance of our nature like a mixture of some frailties; it is by them we are best told that we must not strike too hard upon others, because we ourselves do so often deserve blows; they pull our rage by the sleeve and whisper gentleness to us in our censures, even when they are rightly applied. The faults and passions of husbands bring them down to you, and make them content to live upon less unequal terms than faultless men would be willing to stoop to; so haughty is mankind (as opposed to womankind) till humbled by common weaknesses and defects, which in our corrupted state contribute more towards the reconciling us one to another than all the precepts of the philosophers and divines.

Halifax: *Advice to a Daughter*

To Lord Lansdowne

Do what you like with the Church, it will never make the slightest alteration in my respect and regard for you. All that I require is full permission in shilling pamphlets to protest that we are the most injured, persecuted, and ill-treated persons on the face of the Earth. Against Lord Holland and you personally I could not, and would not, write a single syllable, and of course you must both laugh at such nonsense as I put forth from time to time.

To Monckton Milnes

You do me justice in acknowledging that I have spoken much good of you. I have laughed at you for those follies which I have told you of to your face; but nobody has more loudly and more constantly asserted that you were a very agreeable, clever man, with a very good heart, unimpeachable in all the relations of life, and that you amply deserved to be retained in the place to which you have too hastily elevated yourself by manners unknown to our cold and phlegmatic people.

I thank you for what you say of my good-humour. Lord Dudley, when I took leave of him, said to me, "You have been laughing at me for the last seven years, and you never said anything that I wished unsaid." This pleased me.

From the Letters of Sydney Smith

And even though they [the Greeks] should lay aside their aims and act peaceably, another war falling on the soul, which is not public but private, and which brings with it neither fire nor sword, nor a fleet of ships, nor horses, but is destitute of all these; this war injures the soul, and besieging, fills it with envy, anger, rage, contumely, and ten thousand other evils.

Where then shall any one turn himself, and what truce shall he find? What Olympian, what Nemean league? The Athenian Dionysia and Panathenae are indeed beautiful; but they celebrate these festivals hating and being hated. You speak of a war and not a festival . . . I cannot believe in the festival till I see that those are friends by whom it is celebrated. This is the law and manner of a true league, arranged by the legislator divinity, without the possession of which friendship cannot be seen, not even though a man should frequently make libations, not though he should frequently be enrolled among the Olympian, Isthmean, and Nemean conquerors . . . as long as the war in the soul is without a truce the soul remains without friendship, hostile and sorrowful. These are avenging daemons, these are the furies. . . . Let us call in Philosophy: she will come, she will bring with her the reconciling league, she will proclaim peace.

Maximus of Tyre: *Dissertations*

As touching leagues, which in other places between country and country be so oft concluded, broken and renewed, they never make none with any nation. For to what purpose serve leagues? say they. As though nature had not set sufficient love between man and man. And who so regardeth not nature, think you that he will pass for words? . . . Howbeit, they think that though leagues be never so faithfully observed and kept, yet the custom of making leagues was very evil begun. For this causeth men (as though nations which be separate asunder, by the space of a little hill or a river, were coupled together by no society or bond of nature) to think themselves born adversaries and enemies one to another, and that it were lawful for the one to seek the death and destruction of the other, if leagues were not; . . . But they be of a contrary opinion. That is, that no man ought to be counted an enemy which hath done no injury. And that the fellowship of nature is a strong league; and that men be better and more surely knit together by love and benevolence, than by covenants of leagues; by hearty affection of mind, than by words.

Sir Thomas More: *Utopia*

A political society is to be considered well-ordered, beneficial and in keeping with human dignity if it is grounded on truth. As the Apostle Paul exhorts us: "Away with falsehood then; let everyone speak out the truth to his neighbour; membership of the body binds us to one another." This demands that reciprocal rights and duties be sincerely recognized. Furthermore, human society will be such as We have just described it, if the citizens, guided by justice, apply themselves seriously to respecting the rights of others and discharging their own duties; if they are moved by such fervour of charity as to make their own the needs of others and share with others their own goods: if, finally, they work for a progressively closer fellowship in the world of spiritual values. Human society is realized in freedom, that is to say, in ways and means in keeping with the dignity of its citizens, who accept the responsibility of their actions, precisely because they are by nature rational beings.

Pope John XXIII: *Pacem in Terris*

Above all things never compel your subjects to change their religion. No human power can force the impenetrable intrenchments of liberty in the human heart. Force can never persuade men, it can only make hypocrites. When kings interfere with religion, instead of protecting it they only enslave it. Grant to all religions a political toleration; not equally approving of all, as if you were indifferent, but patiently allowing all that God allows and endeavouring to lead men by gentle persuasion.

Fénelon's advice to the Chevalier St. George

We have a form of government . . . which, because in the administration it hath respect not to the few but to the multitude, is called democracy. Wherein there is not only an equality amongst all men in point of law for their private controversies, but in election to public offices we consider neither class nor rank. . . . Moreover this liberty which we enjoy in the administration of the state, we use also with one another in our daily course of life, neither quarrelling with our neighbour for following his own humour, nor casting on him censorious looks, which, tho' they be no punishment, yet they grieve. So that conversing among ourselves without private offence, we stand chiefly in fear to transgress against the public.

Thucydides

There is another offence unto charity, which no author hath ever written of, and few take notice of; and that is the reproach, not of whole professions, mysteries, and conditions, but of whole nations; wherein by opprobrious epithets we miscall each other, and by an uncharitable logic, from a disposition in a few, conclude a habit in all.

> Le mutin Anglois, et le bravache Ecossois;
> Le bougre Italien, et le fol François;
> Le poltron Romain, le larron de Gascogne,
> L'Espagnol superbe, et l'Alleman yvrogne.

St. Paul, that calls the Cretans liars, doth it but indirectly, and upon quotation of their own poet. It is as bloody a thought in one way as Nero's was in another. For by a word we wound a thousand, and at one blow assassinate the honour of a nation.

Sir Thomas Browne: *Religio Medici*

> For forms of Government let fools contest.
> What e'er is best administer'd is best:
> For modes of faith let graceless zealots fight;
> His can't be wrong whose life is in the right.
> In faith and hope the world will disagree,
> But all mankind's concern is charity:
> All must be false that thwarts this one great end;
> And all of God, that bless mankind or mend.

Pope: *Essay on Man*

Pennsylvania, the Peaceful Colony

William Penn, the Quaker, was granted land in the New World by King Charles II in return for a large sum of money which the King owed him. It was called Sylvania because of its forests and the King insisted on adding the name Penn. The Charter of Pennsylvania empowered Penn to make war on the Indian savages, but Penn refused to build any forts or to have cannon or soldiers in his province.

It was prophesied that all his settlements would soon be destroyed. But Penn took no notice of these prophecies. He set about founding his capital city which he named Philadelphia, the City of Brotherly Love. He made friends with the Indians and they arranged that all quarrels should be settled by a meeting of six white men and six red men. The Indians enjoyed equal citizenship with the white men and an equal choice of land. When William Penn died they mourned him as their friend.

After Penn's death, while every other colony in the New World was constantly attacked by the Indians, Pennsylvania was perfectly free from attack as long as they refused to arm themselves. Many years later the Quakers were outvoted in the State and the colony gave way to pressure on them from the other States and began to spend money in building forts and to train soldiers against possible aggression. They were immediately attacked.

E. B. Emmott: compiled from *The Story of Quakerism*

This was the fullness of time, when Christ Jesus did come, that the Messiah should come.

It was so to the Jews, and it was so to the Gentiles too . . . Christ has excommunicated no nation, no shire, no house, no man: he gives none of his ministers leave to say to any man, thou art not redeemed; he gives no wounded nor afflicted conscience leave to say to itself, I am not redeemed.

Donne: *Sermons*

The brotherhood of man is the teaching of the first two chapters of the book of Genesis. What is new in the teaching of Jesus is again that he lifts the fact of human brotherhood to the level of intention. That all men are of one blood as the children of Adam is mere fact. What matters is the restoration of this unity of fact at the level of personality, as a matter of intention. St. Paul puts this neatly by saying, "As in Adam all die, even so in Christ shall all be made alive." It is the resurrection of the original community of mankind that is the work of Jesus. The separation of peoples, with its nationalism, racial exclusiveness and claims of superiority is an expression of the refusal of man to will his own nature. It makes no difference to the fact that mankind is a unity. The existing diversity of exclusive groups exhibits man's estrangement from himself, his denial of the truth about himself. To accept the truth is to intend the unity of mankind and so to re-establish it as the expression of a human will which has become reconciled to the will of God; it is to make this the goal of human activity. For the religious consciousness, with its unity of theory and practice, the assertion of such a truth is a call to action. Jesus' proclamation of the community of mankind is primarily a call to his own people to accept as their mission, for which in the purpose of God their whole history had been a preparation, the task of breaking down the exclusive nationalism and racialism of the world, and becoming the means of the unification of mankind. It is this that St. Paul expresses when he says that in Christ "there is neither Greek nor Jew, barbarian, Scythian, bond nor free".

John Macmurray: *The Clue to History*

The Grand Rabbin of Lyons was a Jewish chaplain to the French forces in the 1914-1918 war. One day a wounded man staggered into a trench and told the Rabbi that a Roman Catholic was on the point of death in no-man's-land, and was begging that his padre should come to him with a crucifix. The padre could not quickly be found. The Jew rapidly improvised a cross, ran out with it into no-man's-land, and was seen to hold it before the dying man's eyes. He was almost immediately shot by a sniper; the bodies of the Catholic and the Jew were found together.

Victor Gollancz: *A Year of Grace*

Where there is neither Greek nor Jew, circumcision nor uncircumcision, Barbarian, Scythian, bond nor free: but Christ is all in all.

Put on therefore, as the elect of God, holy and beloved, bowels of mercies, kindness, humbleness of mind, meekness, long-suffering;

Forbearing one another, and forgiving one another, if any man have a quarrel against any: even as Christ forgave you, so also do ye.

Colossians

III

Pure Love and Undefiled—Forgiveness

Mutual Forgiveness of each vice
Such are the Gates of Paradise.
Against the Accuser's chief desire
Who walked among the Stones of Fire.

William Blake

To say therefore that vengeance is to be reserved to God is only saying in other words that all the evils in nature are to be reserved and turned over to the Love of God, to be healed by this goodness.

William Law

Forgiveness is the action which lets the other find sympathy where he expected hatred, generosity where he expected retribution, which gives much because it expects much, which recreates new opportunities for the other, because it apprehends the world as a vast bundle of opportunities.

Werner Pelz

Before the duel
THE
ONLOOKER: Let them fight it out, friend! things have gone too far.
God must judge the couple! leave them as they are.

*

Why, you would not bid men, sunk in such a slough,
Strike no aim out further, stick and stink as now.

After the duel
THE
VICTOR: Take the cloak from his face, and at first
Let the corpse do its worst.
How he lies in his rights of a man!
Death has done all death can.
And, absorbed in the new life he leads,
He seeks not, he heeds
Nor his wrong nor my vengeance—both strike
On his senses alike,
And are lost in the solemn and strange
Surprise of the change.
Ha, what avails death to erase
His offence, my disgrace?
I would we were boys as of old
In the field, by the fold:
His outrage, God's patience, man's scorn
Were so easily borne.

I stand here now, he lies in his place:
Cover the face.

Browning: *Before & After*

After a while Martin saw an apple-woman stop just in front of his window. She had a large basket, but there did not seem to be many apples left in it; she had evidently sold most of her stock. On her back she had a sack full of chips, which she was taking home. . . . The sack evidently hurt her, and she wanted to shift it from one shoulder to the other, so she put it down on the footpath and, placing her basket on a post, began to shake down the chips in the sack. While she was doing this a boy in a tattered cap ran up, snatched an apple out of the basket, and tried to slip away; but the old woman noticed it, and turning, caught the boy by his sleeve. . . . Martin dropped his awl, not waiting to stick it in its place, and rushed out of the door. Stumbling up the steps, and dropping his spectacles in his hurry, he ran out into the street. The old woman was pulling the boy's hair and scolding him, and threatening to take him to the police. The lad was struggling and protesting, saying, "I did not take it. What are you beating me for? Let me go!"

Martin separated them. He took the boy by the hand and said, "Let him go, Granny. Forgive him for Christ's sake."

"I'll pay him out, so that he won't forget it for a year! I'll take the rascal to the police!"

Martin began entreating the old woman.

"Let him go, Granny. He won't do it again. Let him go for Christ's sake!"

The old woman let go, and the boy wished to rush away, but Martin stopped him.

"Ask the Granny's forgiveness!" said he. "And don't do it another time. I saw you take the apple."

The boy began to cry and to beg pardon.

"That's right. And now here's an apple for you," and Martin took an apple from the basket and gave it to the boy, saying, "I will pay you, Granny."

"You will spoil them that way, the young rascals," said the old woman. "He ought to be whipped so that he should remember it for a week."

"Oh, Granny, Granny," said Martin, "that's our way—but it's not God's way. If he should be whipped for stealing an apple, what should be done to us for our sins?"

The old woman was silent.

And Martin told her the parable of the lord who forgave his servant a large debt, and how the servant went out and seized his debtor by the throat. The old woman listened to it all, and the boy, too, stood by and listened.

"God bids us forgive," said Martin, "or else we shall not be forgiven. Forgive every one; and a thoughtless youngster most of all."

The old woman wagged her head and sighed.

"It's true enough," said she, "but they are getting terribly spoilt."

"Then we old ones must show them better ways," Martin replied.

"That's just what I say," said the old woman. "I have had seven of them myself, and only one daughter is left." And the old woman began to tell how and where she was living with her daughter, and how many grandchildren she had.

"There now," she said, "I have but little strength left, yet I work hard for the sake of my grandchildren; and nice children they are, too. No one comes out to meet me but the children." And the old woman completely softened at the thought.

"Of course, it was only his childishness, God help him," said she, referring to the boy.

As the old woman was about to hoist her sack on her back, the lad sprang forward to her, saying, "Let me carry it for you, Granny. I'm going that way."

The old woman nodded her head, and put the sack on the boy's back, and they went down the street together, the old woman quite forgetting to ask Martin to pay for the apple. Martin stood and watched them as they went along talking to each other.

Leo Tolstoy: *Where Love is, God is*

William the Silent and Anna of Saxony

When William the Silent's deplorable second wife, Anna of Saxony, decamped with a lawyer from Antwerp he refused to revenge his honour though everyone including the guilty couple expected him to do so as a matter of course. The lawyer's wronged wife pleaded for her husband's life. William granted both life and liberty. Seldom has tolerance paid such tangible and obvious dividends. The couple settled down together again and a son was born of the re-union who grew up to become the painter Peter Paul Rubens.

Compiled from *William the Silent* by V. Wedgewood

Jean Renoir in his recent memoir tells a story of his father, Auguste Renoir, the artist, who was one of the most tolerant and generous minded of men. When, as happened more than once, a friend took advantage of this and stole a painting or two from him, Renoir alluded to the lapse as an error or accident. Once, before leaving Paris with his family for the country, Renoir left the key of his house with a neighbour, asking him to look in and see that all was well every now and again while he was away. On the family's return, they found that the friend had left Paris suddenly, asking someone else to hand back the key. Soon after, fifty or so canvases were discovered to be missing. Renoir was chiefly concerned lest the unfinished pictures might be completed by a forger so he wrote to the friend who, thinking that it was wiser, returned, and with tears confessed to the theft and that the canvases were already sold. He pleaded his poverty. Renoir told him to forget about it, as if the pictures were sold nothing could be done as neither of them had the money to buy them back. He tried to stop the man's overpowering gratitude and sent him off as soon as possible, actually giving him all the money he had in the house at the time. He and his wife then agreed to tell nobody in case of disgracing the man, whose father was a magistrate.

Compiled from *My Father* by Jean Renoir

[A legend of Sengai, the Japanese Buddhist monk and artist.]

When Sengai was Abbot of the Zen monastery at Shofukuji, one of his young disciples often used to climb over the monastery walls in order to spend the night in freedom. One morning, as day dawned, he was climbing back when, instead of the rock which he used as a foothold, he stepped upon a warm soft object. He jumped quietly from it to the ground and turning, saw it was his master, Sengai, crouched low to provide a safe foothold for the truant. The young monk was terribly ashamed but his master only seemed anxious lest he might have come to some harm and mildly told him to go back quietly to his cell. The disciple never forgot this gentle tolerance and he himself grew to be a fine and holy man.

Compiled from the Introduction to the Catalogue of Sengai's pictures, sponsored by the Arts Council in 1963

Diderot and the satirist

There came to him one morning a young man bringing a manuscript in his hand. He begged Diderot to do him the favour of reading it, and to make any remarks he might think useful on the margin. Diderot found it to be a bitter satire upon his own person and writings. On the young man's return, Diderot asked him his grounds for making such an attack. "I am without bread," the satirist answered, "and I hoped you might perhaps give me a few crowns not to print it." Diderot at once forgot everything in pity for the starving scribbler. "I will tell you a way of making more than that by it. The brother of the Duke of Orleans is one of the pious, and he hates me. Dedicate your satire to him, get it bound with his arms on the cover; take it to him some fine morning, and you will certainly get assistance from him." "But I don't know the prince, and the dedicatory epistle embarrasses me." "Sit down," said Diderot, "and I will write one for you." The dedication was written, the author carried it to the prince, and received a handsome fee.

John Morley: *Diderot*

[Mr. Bulstrode, a strict evangelical Pillar of Society in Middlemarch, has been threatened with the exposure of a dishonest and disreputable past by a blackmailer. The secret has leaked out and has been revealed to his hitherto trusting and admiring wife by the neighbours.]

She locked herself in her room. She needed time to get used to her maimed consciousness, her poor lopped life, before she could walk steadily to the place allotted her. . . . Her honest ostentatious nature made the sharing of a merited dishonour as bitter as it could be to any mortal.

But this imperfectly-taught woman, whose phrases and habits were an odd patchwork, had a loyal spirit within her. The man whose prosperity she had shared through nearly half a life, and who had unvaryingly cherished her—now that punishment had befallen him it was not possible to her in any sense to forsake him. There is a forsaking which still sits at the same board and lies on the same couch with the forsaken soul, withering it the more by unloving proximity. She knew, when she locked her door, that she should unlock it ready to go down to her unhappy husband and espouse his sorrow, and say of his guilt, I will mourn and not reproach. . . .

Bulstrode, who knew that his wife had been out and had come in saying that she was not well, had spent the time in an agitation equal to hers. He had looked forward to her learning the truth from others, and had acquiesced in that probability, as something easier to him than any confession. But now that he imagined the moment of her knowledge come, he awaited the result in anguish. His daughters had been obliged to consent to leave him, and though he had allowed some food to be brought to him, he had not touched it. He felt himself perishing slowly in unpitied misery. Perhaps he should never see his wife's face with affection in it again. And if he turned to God there seemed to be no answer but the pressure of retribution.

It was eight o'clock in the evening before the door opened and his wife entered. He dared not look up at her. He sat with his eyes bent down, and as she went towards him she thought he looked smaller—he seemed so withered and shrunken. A movement of new compassion and old tenderness went through her like a great wave, and putting one hand on his which rested on the arm of the chair, and the other on his shoulder, she said, solemnly but kindly—

"Look up, Nicholas."

He raised his eyes with a little start and looked at her half amazed for a moment: her pale face, her changed, mourning dress, the trembling about her mouth, all said, "I know"; and her hands and eyes rested gently on him. He burst out crying and they cried together, she sitting at his side. They could not yet speak to each other of the shame which she was bearing with him, or of the acts which had brought it down on them. His confession was silent, and her promise of faithfulness was silent.

George Eliot: *Middlemarch*

I confess, my God, that I have long been, and even now am, recalcitrant to the love of my neighbour. Just as much as I have derived intense joy in the superhuman delight of dissolving myself and losing myself in the souls for which I was destined by the mysterious affinities of human love, so I have always felt an inborn hostility to, and closed myself to, the common run of those whom You tell me to love. I find no difficulty in integrating into my inward life everything above and beneath me (in the same line as me, as it were) in the universe—whether matter, plants, animals; and then powers, dominions and angels: these I can accept without difficulty and delight to feel myself sustained within their hierarchy. But "the other man", my God—by which I do not mean "the poor, the halt, the lame and the sick", but "the other" quite simply as "other", the one who seems to exist independently of me because his universe seems closed to mine, and who seems to shatter the unity and the silence of the world for me—would I be sincere if I did not confess that my instinctive reaction is to rebuff him? and that the mere thought of entering into spiritual communication with him disgusts me?

Grant, O God, that the light of Your countenance may shine for me in the life of that "other". . . . Grant that I may see You, even and above all, in the souls of my brothers, at their most personal, and most true, and most distant. . . . Jesus, Saviour of human activity to which You have given meaning, Saviour of human suffering to which You have given living value be also the Saviour of human unity; compel us to discard our pettinesses, and to venture forth, resting upon You, into the uncharted ocean of charity.

Pierre Teilhard de Chardin: *Le Milieu Divin*

[Dirk Coornhert was driven into exile because, at Haarlem, in 1576, he dared to preach tolerance to Catholics and Calvinists alike. He was forced to publish his book on ethics—"the Wellevenskunste" (the art of living)—anonymously. The following passage is taken from the chapter on long-suffering, but tolerance permeates all his work.]

Long-suffering is cool and quenches the fiery heat of hasty anger. For where cold enters, heat must depart. Bitter anger destroys but sweet long-suffering is wholesome. Long-suffering is active where there are those who strive for the hurt and destruction of others.

God has no part in hatred or destruction but He can teach us long-suffering through them. The wise man understands that God is over all and through all and thus he does not become angry with those who serve God indirectly by providing him with the means of possessing his soul in long-suffering patience.

Moreover, the wise pity those who wish them ill, for they remember when they lacked wisdom and offended others and how they then wished to be treated with long-suffering themselves; so they do as they would be done by and tolerate the weakness of those who treat them badly.

Translated by Jennifer Thomassen

All acts of forbearance or of pardon are . . . acts forced from one by sincerity towards oneself. I must practise unlimited forgiveness because, if I did not, I should be wanting in sincerity to myself, for it would be acting as if I myself were not guilty in the same way as the other has been guilty towards me. Because my life is so liberally spotted with falsehood, I must forgive falsehood which has been practised upon me; because I myself have been in so many cases wanting in love, and guilty of hatred, slander, deceit, or arrogance, I must pardon any want of love, and all hatred, slander, deceit, or arrogance which have been directed against myself. I must forgive quietly and unostentatiously; in fact I do not really pardon at all, for I do not let things develop to any such act of *judgement*. . . . We have to carry on the struggle against the evil that is in mankind, not by judging others, but by judging ourselves. Struggle with oneself and veracity towards oneself are the means by which we influence others. . . . It is not from kindness to others that I am gentle, peaceable, forbearing, and friendly, but because by such behaviour I prove my own profoundest Self-realization to be true. Reverence for life which I apply to my own existence, and reverence for life which keeps me in a temper of devotion to other existence than my own, interpenetrate each other.

Albert Schweitzer: *Civilization and Ethics*

[In a Russian Prison.]

Strangely enough, in this place which is one of the subtlest Palaces of Torture, most of the jailors are genuinely kind. Yet they must be staunch communists, proved Stalinites, to be here at all. They are certainly made to believe that we prisoners are all self-interested haters of freedom and progress. Can human nature be so near the divine after all, that even under such awful conditions more kindness than cruelty flows from man to man? . . .

The sad young jailor is back in my cell again—"You must clean this place thoroughly now* . . . There is no brush, you'll have to use your hands, and those bits of rag. Everything has got to be left perfectly clean."

* This included an "indescribably filthy" lavatory pan.

Pink and unhappy, he keeps his head slightly averted.

"May I wash myself properly, not hurriedly, when I've done all this?"

His head swings round. Facing me, he exclaims—"Of course, *of course*!"—in a voice so eager that it is almost grateful.

[The senior jailor discovers that the prisoner cannot eat black bread without becoming ill.]

"I shall see what I can do . . . But you must never refuse your ration again."

Proud and important he goes out.

Ridiculous creature! Yet . . . kind. In another environment, at home with his wife and children, he could possibly be irritating and somewhat comic, but certainly very kind. . . . Is that not the one thing that matters above all? Indiscriminate, all-pervading kindness? Kindness as a mood of approach to everyone . . . except the cads and bullies. . . . And why such an exception? Should kindness not be as indiscriminate as the sun? And what about the devilish cruelty. . . . It is unpardonable that anyone should be tortured, even you—if *you* merely leave it at that. But, surely, when you overcome the pain inflicted on you by them, you make *their* criminal record less villainous? . . . But when, through weakness, cowardice, lack of balance, lack of serenity, you augment your pain, their crime becomes so much the darker, and it is darkened by you. If you could understand this, your making yourself invulnerable would not be *only* an act of self-preservation, it would be a kindness to Them. . . . Look down right into the depths of your heart and tell me—Is it not right for you to be kind to them? Even to them? Particularly to them, perhaps? Is it not right that those men who have no kindness within them should get a surplus of it flowing towards them from without? The whole of me responds with a "Yes"! like a throb of thundering music. It is so shattering that it makes me stagger. The jailor steadies me: "Take care!" He looks concerned, he has the gentle eyes of a puppy. "All right?" "Yes" and we move on. . . .

Julia de Beausobre: *The Woman Who Could Not Die*

ANTIGONE Nevertheless, these rites are due
To the underworld.

CREON But not in equal measure
Both for the good man and the bad.

ANTIGONE Who knows
This is not virtue there?

CREON The enemy
Can never be a friend, even in death.

ANTIGONE Well, I was made for fellowship in love,
Not fellowship in hate.

Sophocles: *Antigone*

To see the universal and all-pervading Spirit of Truth face to face one must be able to love the meanest of creation as oneself. And a man who aspires after that cannot afford to keep out of any field of life. . . . Identification with everything that lives is impossible without self-purification. . . . But the path of self-purification is hard and steep. . . . To conquer the subtle passions seems to me to be harder far than the physical conquest of the world by force of arms. Ever since my return to India I have had experiences of the dormant passions lying hidden within me. The knowledge of them has made me feel humiliated though not defeated. . . . But I know that I have still before me a difficult path to traverse. . . . So long as a man does not of his own free will put himself last among his fellow creatures, there is no salvation for him.

Gandhi: *An Autobiography*

Remember particularly that you cannot be a judge of any one. For no one can judge a criminal, until he recognises that he is just such a criminal as the man standing before him, and that he perhaps is more than all men to blame for that crime. When he understands that, he will be able to be a judge. Though that sounds absurd, it is true. If I had been righteous myself, perhaps there would have been no criminal standing before me. If you can take upon yourself the crime of the criminal your heart is judging, take it at once, suffer for him yourself, and let him go without reproach. And even if the law itself makes you his judge, act in the same spirit so far as possible, for he will go away and condemn himself more bitterly than you have done. If, after your kiss, he goes away untouched, mocking at you, do not let that be a stumbling-block to you. It shows his time has not yet come, but it will come in due course. And if it come not, no matter; if not he, then another in his place will understand and suffer, and judge and condemn himself, and the truth will be fulfilled. Believe that, believe it without doubt; for in that lies all the hope and faith of the saints. . . .

If the evil doing of men moves you to indignation and overwhelming distress, even to a desire for vengeance on the evildoers, shun above all things that feeling. Go at once and seek suffering for yourself, as though you were yourself guilty of that wrong. Accept that suffering and bear it and your heart will find comfort, and you will understand that you too are guilty, for you might have been a light to the evil-doers, even as the one man sinless, and you were not a light to them. If you had been a light, you would have lightened the path for others too, and the evil-doer might perhaps have been saved by your light from his sin. And even though your light was shining, yet you see men were not saved by it, hold firm and doubt not the power of the heavenly light. Believe that if they were not saved, they will be saved hereafter. And if they are not saved hereafter, then their sons will be saved, for your light will not die even when you are dead. The righteous man departs, but his light remains. Men are always saved after the death of the deliverer. Men reject their prophets and slay them, but they love their martyrs and honour those whom they have slain. You are working for the whole, you are acting for the future.

Fyodor Dostoevsky: *The Brothers Karamazov*

"Love your enemies!" Mark you, not simply those who happen not to be your friends, but your enemies, your positive and active enemies. Either this is a mere Oriental hyperbole, a bit of verbal extravagance, meaning only that we should, as far as we can, abate our animosities, or else it is sincere and literal. Outside of certain cases of intimate individual relation, it seldom has been taken literally. Yet it makes one ask the question: Can there in general be a level of emotion so unifying, so obliterative of differences between man and man, that even enmity may come to be an irrelevant circumstance and fail to inhibit the friendlier interests aroused?... Psychologically and in principle, the precept "Love your enemies" is not self-contradictory. It is merely the extreme limit of a kind of magnanimity with which, in the shape of pitying tolerance of our oppressors, we are fairly familiar. Yet if radically followed, it would involve such a breach with our instinctive springs of action as a whole, and with the present world's arrangements, that a critical point would practically be passed, and we should be born into another kingdom of being.

William James: *The Varieties of Religious Experience*

And yet I will my thoughts suppress
And keep my tongue from censure clear,
The Jew, the Turk, the heathen bless
And hold the plough and persevere.

There's God in ev'ry man most sure
And every soul's to Christ allied,
If fear deject, if hopes allure,
If Jesus wept, and pay'd and died.

To give my brother more than due
In talent or in name;
Nor e'en mine enemy pursue
To hurt or to defame.

Nay more, to bless him and to pray
Mine anger to control;
And give the wages of the day
To him that hunts my soul.

Christopher Smart: *Poems*

I did not think he ought to be shut up. His infirmities were not noxious to society. He insisted on people praying with him; and I'd as lief pray with Kit Smart as anyone else. Another charge was, that he did not love clean linen; and I have no passion for it.

Dr. Johnson on Christopher Smart, from Boswell's *Life of Johnson*

When someone may do you an injury, or speak ill of you, remember that he either does it or speaks it believing that it is right and meet for him to do so. It is not possible, then, that he can follow the thing that appears to you but the thing that appears to him. Wherefore, if it appear evil to him, it is he that is injured, being deceived. For also if anyone should take a true consequence to be false, it is not the consequence that is injured, but he which is deceived. Setting out then from these opinions, you will bear a gentle mind towards any man who may revile you. For say on each occasion, so it appeared to him.

Epictetus

Come make peace with the Cavaliers, your enemies, and let them have a livelihood, and love your enemies, and do to them as you would have had them do to you . . . Let them go in peace, and let love wear the crown . . . Their persons are part of the creation as well as you.

Gerard Winstanley

Lord Falkland and the Civil War

At Edgehill, when the Enemy was rowted, he was like to have incurred greate perill by interposinge to save those who had throwne away ther armes and against whome it may be others were more fierce for ther havinge throwne them away, insomuch as a man might thinke, he came into the Field only out of curiosity to see the face of danger, and charity to praevent the sheddinge of bloode. . . . From the entrance into this unnaturall warr, his naturall cheerefulnesse and vivacity grew clouded, and a kind of sadnesse and dejection of Spiritt stole upon him, which he had never bene used to . . . and after . . . the furious resolution of the two houses, not to admitt any treaty for peace . . . he who had bene so exactly unreserved and affable to all men . . . became on a suddayne lesse communicable, and thene very sadd, pale, and exceedingly affected with the spleene. . . . When there was any overture or hope of peace, he would be more erecte, and vigorous, and exceedingly sollicitous to presse any thinge which he thought might promote it, and sittinge amongst his friends often after a deepe silence, and frequent sighes, would with a shrill and sadd Accent ingeminate the word, Peace, Peace and would passyonately professe that the very Agony of the Warr . . . tooke his sleepe from him, and would shortly breake his hearte.

Clarendon: *Lives*

Jesus does not deny the existence of the enemy, i.e. he does not try to argue us out of our belief that there is such a one. He simply asks us to deny him existence *as* an enemy. We are to see him as just another man we are free to love. He may be the very neighbour we need—the "good" Samaritan—because he compliments us, because he seems so different from us. He is the man who, more than any other, challenges our humanity, discovers us, makes us see what we really are—"sinners who love those who love them". He is the man I most readily condemn and in whom, therefore, I am most clearly condemned, "for the measure you give will be the measure you get back". By judging him I am judged, for by acknowledging him as my enemy I compel him to acknowledge me as his and to see me as I insist on seeing him.

Werner Pelz: *God is no More*

[Richard Gettner, the deserter, has shot the Countess's son in a duel.]

COUNTESS Corporal, have you children?
1ST GUARD Yes, ma'am, yes.
COUNTESS Would you injure them, to please any opinion?
1ST GUARD Ma'am, that's no question.
COUNTESS Then do not injure
Mine. I mean my son. I ask you
Not to make him the cause of punishment,
Not to make his wound a death,
Not to turn his challenge into a judgment.
The stream of his life is running
Shallow and slowly. Pray for him,
Not because I love him, but because
You are the life you pray for. And because
Richard Gettner is the life you pray for.
And because there is nothing on the earth
Which doesn't happen in your own hearts.

Christopher Fry: *The Dark is Light Enough*

Almighty God, have mercy on N and N and on all that bear me evil will, and would me harm, and their faults and mine together, by such easy, tender, merciful means as Thine infinite wisdom best can divine, vouchsafe to amend and redress, and make us saved souls in heaven together where we may ever live and love together with thee and thy blessed saints, O glorious Trinity, for the bitter passion of our sweet Saviour Christ, amen.

Ascribed to Sir Thomas More

PROSPERO Say, my spirit
How fares the King and 's followers?
ARIEL . . . confin'd together
In the same fashion as you gave in charge:
Just as you left them: all prisoners, sir
In the lime-grove which weather-fends your cell;
. . . Brimful of sorrow and dismay;

. . . Your charm so strongly works them,
That if you now beheld them, your affections
Would become tender.

PROSPERO . . . Dost thou think so, spirit!

ARIEL Mine would, sir, were I human.

PROSPERO And mine shall.
Hast thou, which art but air, a touch, a feeling
Of their afflictions, and shall not myself,
One of their kind, that relish all as sharply,
Passion as they, be kindlier mov'd than thou art?
Though with their high wrongs I am struck to the quick
Yet with my nobler reason 'gainst my fury
Do I take part.

Shakespeare: *The Tempest*

Forgiveness of Sin is only at the Judgement Seat of Jesus the Saviour, where the Accuser is cast out, not because he Sins, but because he torments the Just and makes them do what he condemns as Sin and what he knows is opposite to their own Identity.

It is not because Angels are Holier than Men or Devils that makes them Angels, but because they do not Expect Holiness from one another, but from God only. . . . Angels are happier than Men and Devils because they are not always Prying after Good and Evil in one another.

William Blake: *Vision of Last Judgement*

[William Law lived at a time when belief in everlasting punishment for the majority of mankind was an accepted part of the teaching of the Church. At first Law himself unwillingly subscribed to this. His reluctance may be deduced from his silence on the subject. But towards the end of his life he comes out joyfully upon the side of the heretical doctrine of universalism, going indeed further than most in the following passage where he asserts the final redemption of even the fallen angels.]

With respect to this doctrine of universal redemption I very well remember Mr. William Law's speaking of it, upon my making him the last visit at Easter, 1761, a few days before his death. . . . He said that not only the whole human race but even the fallen angels would all be delivered out of misery. He said that there would be a chasm in the creation without the angels being taken into happiness. But that could not be until they saw the whole creation made happy before them. When they saw this, . . . it would produce the blessed effect of awakening that goodness which laid dormant in them. For though that goodness might be shut up in a sevenfold deeper or stronger compaction than fire is in a flint, yet as it was shut up and preserved in them, it would come forth, and so they also would be made happy, to the full display of God's love and goodness to all His creatures. This was really the substance of what Mr. Law said upon the occasion, and nearly in his own words, according to the best of my remembrance. Mr. Law spoke upon the subject of his own accord, [when] we took a walk through the town of Kings Cliffe. He then opened a gate into a field; it was a rising ground, and then he began the discourse, and spoke like an angel on this and other matters.

John Byrom: *Journal*

Jesus was sitting in Moses' Chair
They brought the trembling Woman there.
Moses commands she be stoned to death,
What was the sound of Jesus' breath?
He laid His hand on Moses Law:
The Ancient Heavens, in Silent Awe
Writ with Curses from Pole to Pole,
All away began to roll:
The Earth trembling and Naked lay
In secret bed of Mortal Clay,

On Sinai felt the hand divine
Putting back the bloody shrine,
And she heard the breath of God
As she heard by Eden's flood;
Good and Evil are no more!
Sinai's trumpets, cease to roar!

William Blake: *Everlasting Gospel*

When Abraham sat at his tent door, according to his custom, waiting to entertain strangers, he espied an old man, stooping and leaning on his staff, weary with age and travail, coming towards him, who was a hundred years of age; he received him kindly, washed his feet, provided supper, caused him to sit down; but observing that the old man ate and prayed not, nor begged a blessing on his meat, he asked him why he did not worship the God of heaven. The old man told him that he worshipped the fire only, and acknowledged no other God. At which answer Abraham grew so zealously angry, that he threw the old man out of his tent, and exposed him to all the evils of the night and an unguarded condition. When the old man was gone, God called to Abraham, and asked him where the stranger was. He replied, "I thrust him away, because he did not worship thee." God answered him, "I have suffered him these hundred years, though he dishonoured me; and wouldst thou not endure him one night?"

Jeremy Taylor: *The Liberty of Prophesying*

"You don't believe in God," Alyosha added, speaking this time very sorrowfully. He fancied besides that his brother was looking at him ironically. "How does your poem end?" he asked, suddenly looking down. "Or was it the end?"

"I meant to end it like this. When the Inquisitor ceased speaking he waited some time for his Prisoner to answer him. His silence weighed down upon him. He saw that the Prisoner had listened intently all the time, looking gently in his face and evidently not wishing to reply. The old man longed for Him to say something however bitter and terrible. But He suddenly approached the old man in silence and softly kissed him on his bloodless aged lips. That was all his answer. The old man shuddered. His lips moved. He went to the door, opened it, and said to Him: "Go, and come no more . . . come not at all, never, never!" And he let Him out into the dark alleys of the town. The Prisoner went away."

"And the old man?"

"The kiss glows in his heart, but the old man adheres to his idea."

Fyodor Dostoevsky: *The Brothers Karamazov*

[The Right Rev. Leonard Wilson, then Bishop of Singapore, speaks of his experiences as a Japanese prisoner.]

In the middle of torture [when] they asked me why I did not curse them I told them that it was because I was a follower of Jesus Christ, who taught us that we were all brethren. I did not like to use the words "Father forgive them". It seemed too blasphemous to use our Lord's words; but I *felt* them, and I said, "Father, I know these men are doing their duty. Help them to see that I am innocent". When I muttered "Forgive them", I wondered how far I was being dramatic, and if I really meant it; because I looked at their faces as they stood round, taking it in turn to flog me, and their faces were hard and cruel, and some of them were evidently enjoying their cruelty. But, by the grace of God, I saw those men not as they were, but as they had been. Once they were little children with their brothers and sisters . . . in those far-off days before they had been conditioned by their false nationalist ideals. And it is hard to hate little children.

So I saw them not as they were, but as they were capable of becoming, redeemed by the power of Christ, and I knew that I should say "Forgive".

From a broadcast given on October 13th, 1946

And it happened to Nekhlyudov as it often happens to men who are living a spiritual life. The thought that at first seemed strange, paradoxical, or even only a jest, being confirmed more and more often by life's experience, suddenly appeared as the simplest, truest certainty. In this way the idea that the only certain means of salvation from the terrible evil from which men are suffering is, that they should always acknowledge themselves to be guilty before God, and therefore unable to punish or reform others, became clear to him. . . . Now he saw clearly whence came all the horrors he had seen, and what ought to be done to put an end to them. The answer he had been unable to find was the same that Christ gave to Peter. It was to forgive always, every one, to forgive an infinite number of times, because there are none who are not themselves guilty, . . . Nekhlyudov now understood that society, and order in general, exist, not thanks to these lawful criminals who judge and punish others, but because notwithstanding their depraving influence men still pity and love one another.

Leo Tolstoy: *Resurrection*

An Indian greeted a soldier who, at the time of the Indian Mutiny, was about to put a bayonet into his body, with the words, "And thou too art divine."

Quoted by Reinhold Niebuhr

One other strange thing. I felt absolutely no hatred. Something happened to my body; it was only the body of a boy, and it reacted as such. But my soul was occupied with something completely different. Of course it noticed the little creatures who were there with my body, but it was filled so with itself that it could not closely concern itself with them.

Since then I have often thought of Jesus. I can well understand the measureless love he felt for all men, and especially for those who took part in driving nails into his hands. From the moment when he left Gethsemane, he stood high above all passion.

Seaman Kim Malthe-Bruun: *Dying We Live*

And when they were come to the place, which is called Calvary, there they crucified him, and the malefactors, one on the right hand and the other on the left.

Then said Jesus, "Father, forgive them; for they know not what they do".

St. Luke

NOTES ON AUTHORS

These notes give basic information on authors who are well known and rather more on those who are lesser known. Further facts and comments also have been added when these have seemed of special interest in their bearing upon the subject of this book—for instance, when they illustrate variety of interests, wide experience, or concern with tolerance or intolerance. The names of those authors about whom information is obviously superfluous have not been included.

Anselm, St. (*1033-1109*). Abbot of Bec. He succeeded Lanfranc as Archbishop of Canterbury. A great scholar and teacher. He opposed the tyranny of William Rufus and was exiled by him. He was a lovable man whose letters and meditations show true humility and sympathy with others.

Asoka (*264-223* B.C.). Ruled over the greater part of India. Refused to carry a victorious campaign to its conclusion because of the destruction it was causing. Left a number of edicts engraved upon rocks.

Bagehot, Walter (*1826-1877*). Banker, economist, man of letters and much else. "You see," he once wrote to a friend, "I have hunting, banking, ships, publishers, an article, and a Christmas to do, all at once, and it is my opinion they will all get muddled. A muddle will *print*, however, though it won't add up—which is the real advantage of literature".

Barbellion, W. N. P. (*Bruce F. Cummings*), (*1890-1919*). Diarist and entomologist. This extract comes from "Enjoying Life" and not from the better known "Journal of a Diappointed Man". It gives an aspect of Barbellion's character often obscured in the Journal by illness.

Baxter, Richard (*1615-1691*). Author of The Saints Rest and several of our best known hymns. A man of moderation in a time of bitter strife, he was consulted both by Cromwell and by Charles II, and refused a pastorship from the one and two bishoprics from the other. Prosecuted under the Act of Uniformity he was condemned to prison by Judge Jeffreys in a notorious trial but was released after two years by James II. His funeral was said to be "a meeting place of opposites".

Beausobre, Julia de (*Lady Namier*), (*contemporary*). She has written of her experience as a prisoner in Russia after the Revolution in a remarkable book *The Woman Who Could Not Die*. She escaped to England and has lived here for many years. She married Sir Lewis Namier, the famous historian.

Beerbohm, Max (*1872-1956*). Caricaturist, essayist and, in his old age, inimitable broadcaster.

Blake, William (*1757-1827*). Engraver, painter, poet, mystic. He had a passionate concern for all the weak and exploited, especially for children and for those who suffered under conditions brought about by the Industrial Revolution.

Booth, Charles (*1840-1916*). Victorian shipowner, cousin by marriage of Beatrice Webb, whom he greatly influenced. He conducted an extensive enquiry into the Life and Labours of the People of London from 1886-1891.

Borelli, Don Mario (*contemporary*). Italian priest and social worker.

Boyle, Robert (*1627-1691*). Physicist and chemist. One of the founder members of the Royal Society. He was also a director of the East India Company, and at his own expense sent out translations of the Bible for distribution. His book *The Sceptical Chymist*, 1661, laid the foundation of modern chemistry.

Brown, John (*1810-1882*). Doctor and author. Best known for his two portraits, of a dog, *Rab and his friends*, and of a child, *Pet Marjorie*. The passages here included are all from his discursive papers *Horae Subsecivae*. He has affinities with Charles Lamb, the same mixture of pathos and humour and quiet scholarship.

Browne, Sir Thomas (1605-1682). He lived quietly and peaceably all through the Civil War, practising his medical profession and writing his beautiful strange books, *Religio Medici* and *Urn Burial*, which were re-discovered by Charles Lamb after a period of almost total oblivion.

Burke, Edmund (1729-1797). Statesman and philosopher. He was a mixture of pronounced tolerance and intolerance. He defended the American Colonies and the Indian natives in some of the finest speeches ever made. He was also tolerant upon Ireland and the Abolition of the Slave Trade. But he was fiercely and implacably opposed to the French Revolution. He was capable of saying that no French prisoners should be taken alive in the subsequent wars, and he helped to suppress freedom of opinion and parliamentary reform at home. This attitude was based on an almost mystical view of tradition and a deep-rooted fear of disruption and sudden change.

Butterfield, Herbert (contemporary). Regius Professor of Modern History at Cambridge.

Caird, John (1820-1898). A great Scottish preacher and professor of Divinity. Principal of Glasgow University.

de Chardin, Pierre Teilhard (1881-1955). Catholic priest and palaeontologist, descended from Voltaire. Travelled widely in China and the deserts of Ordos and Gobi. His books were not allowed to be published during his lifetime and he acquiesced in this prohibition by the Catholic Church with patience and humility.

Chillingworth, William (1602-1643). One of the group of religious thinkers and writers who gathered at Lord Falkland's house at Great Tew in Oxfordshire.

Cicero, Marcus Tullius (*106–48* B.C.). Orator and author. Killed in consequence of his famous speeches against Mark Antony.

Clark, D. Stafford- (*contemporary*). Consultant Physician, Department of Psychological Medicine at Guy's Hospital, and Consultant Physician at Maudsley and Bethlem Royal Hospitals.

Colet, John (*1467–1519*). Friend of Erasmus and Sir Thomas More. He caused a theological revolution by his lectures on St. Paul's Epistles at Oxford. Dean of St. Paul's. Founded St. Paul's School in 1509. Attacked for heresy.

Coornhert, Dirk Volckertzoon (*died 1590*). Dutch preacher and author of many books on religious freedom and mutual tolerance. Persecuted by Catholics and Calvinists alike.

Cowper, William (*1731–1800*). A gentle revolutionary in political principles and literary practice. Best known for his hymns, his long meditative poem *The Task* and his ballad of John Gilpin.

Crabbe, George (*1754–1832*). Suffolk poet, best remembered today as the creator of "Peter Grimes", a character in his poem *The Village*. Jane Austen said he was the only man she could have married. He was desperately poor until generously befriended by Edmund Burke.

Culverwel, Nathaniel (*died about 1651*). One of the Cambridge Platonists. His most famous work, *Light of Nature*, was published the year after his death.

Day, Thomas (*1748–1789*). Author of *Sandford and Merton* and *The Dying Negro*. Friend of Richard Edgeworth (Maria Edgeworth's father). He was a humourless but sincere educationist and philanthropist.

Defoe, Daniel (*1659 or 60–1731*). Author and political satirist. He suffered in the pillory and in prison for his defence of Dissenters. An indefatigable writer, both in prison and out, upon every conceivable subject, he is remembered now chiefly for the immortal works *Moll Flanders* and *Robinson Crusoe*, but his most important contemporary achievement was his newspaper *The Review*.

De Sales, St. Francis (1567-1622). He abandoned the prospects of a great worldly career for the Church. He was appointed Bishop of Geneva, and established a congregation of nuns under Madame de Chantal, to whom he wrote numerous letters. Canonized in 1665.

Diderot, Denis (1713-1784). His *Pensées Philosophiques* was publicly burned and he was imprisoned for his *Lettre sur les Aveugles*. He is best known for his *Cyclopaedia*, for which he gathered together most of the oustanding French writers of the time. The work was far more than an Encyclopaedia and was prohibited as anti-clerical. He was called an atheist but was certainly a great humanist and a brilliant critic.

Dolci, Danilo (contemporary). Italian social reformer. Went to Sicily in 1952 and lived among the very poor there. Since then he has dedicated himself to their service.

Dostoevsky, Fyodor (1821-1881). Russian novelist. Condemned to death as a revolutionist. Reprieved at the last moment, he was sent to Siberia for ten years.

Elstob, Elizabeth (1683-1756). The first woman to study Anglo-Saxon, "and", remarked a near contemporary, "I suppose also the last". She published a translation of the *Homily of St. Gregory* and a grammar, and edited the Saxon Homilies, but this work remained in manuscript and, together with other books and papers, was lost. She was reduced to great poverty, but eventually she became governess to the Duke of Portland's children. "If women may be said to have souls," she wrote "and that their souls are their better part, and that what is Best deserves our greatest Care for its Improvement; furthermore if good Learning be one of the Soul's greatest Improvements . . . where is the Fault in Women's seeking after learning? Why are they not to be valu'd for acquiring to themselves the noblest Ornaments?"

Epictetus (*born about* A.D. *50*). A Stoic philosopher who had been a slave in Rome. He left no works, but his sayings were collected and written down by his pupil Arrian.

Erasmus (*1457-1536*). Scholar and humanist friend of More, Fisher and Colet. "A prophet without sackcloth and a reformer untouched by heat or fury."

Eusobius. Late Ionic Platonist.

Falkland, Viscount (*1610-1643*). A reluctant supporter of Charles I. Secretary of State. Killed at Battle of Newbury.

Faraday, Michael (*1791-1867*). A great discoverer whose work on electricity was the basis of a new science. He was also an outstanding teacher and lecturer.

Fénelon, François de Salignac (*1651-1715*). Wrote his *De L'Education des Filles* when Director of an Institute for women converts to Catholicism. He incurred the anger of Louis XIV by his satire *Télémaque* and was banished from Paris.

Forster, E. M. (*contemporary*). Novelist and essayist.

Fox, Charles James (*1749-1806*). Statesman. He strove all his life for unpopular causes—Catholic Emancipation, Parliamentary Reform, Self-government for Ireland and the aboliton of the Slave Trade. He was personally exceedingly loved by a wide circle of friends and relatives.

Fox, George (*1624-1690*). Founder of the Society of Friends. A mystic and revolutionary thinker, he was moved to protest against all formalism in religion. The doctrine of the Inner Light was the foundation of his teaching.

Fry, Christopher (*contemporary*). Dramatist.

Fuller, Thomas (*1608-1661*). Chaplain to the Royalist forces and for their comfort wrote in 1645 *Good Thoughts in Bad Times*, followed in 1647 by *Good Thoughts in Worse Times*. In 1655 he published a Church History of Britain which was attacked for partiality to Puritanism. At the Restoration he was appointed Chaplain to Charles II. His best known work is his *Worthies of England*, which, though he was twenty years writing it, remained unfinished at his death. It is a sort of grand English Baedeker and *Who's Who* in one, written in a witty, vivid and enchanting style.

Gandhi, Mahatma (1869–1948). Practised law in South Africa for seventeen years. In 1915 he returned to India and gave up the rest of his life to working for India's freedom and for the welfare of the Indian peasant. His preaching of non-violent resistance had widespread results.

Greville, Charles (1794–1865). Author of the Greville Memoirs, now published for first time in their entirety. They consist of voluminous diaries, a wonderful commentary on the fashionable political life of his times.

Grimble, Arthur (1888–1956). District Officer of the Gilbert and Ellis Islands, Governor of the Windward Islands.

Halifax, George Savile, Marquis of (1633–1695). President of the Council at accession of James II but dismissed for opposition to repeal of Test and Habeus Corpus Acts. Resumed office, under William and Mary. A witty and pleasant character.

Harvey, William (1578–1657). Discoverer of the circulation of the blood. Physician to James I and Charles I. Aubrey tells a nice story of him at the battle of Edgehill. "During the fight the Prince and the Duke of York were committed to Harvey's care. He told me that he withdrew with them under a hedge, and took out of his pocket a book and read. But he had not read very long before a bullet of a great gun grazed on the ground near him, which made him remove his station."

Heath, R. F. (contemporary). Warden of an interdenominational community engaged in religious and social work.

Herbert, George (1593-1633). Scholar, musician, clergyman and poet. The best account of him is to be found in Izaak Walton's *Lives* which well illustrates his love of tolerance.

Hill, A. V. (contemporary). Physiologist and bio-physicist. Nobel Prize for Medicine, 1922. Rescued many scientists in Germany and Austria from Nazi persecution.

Hoggart, Richard (contemporary). Professor of English at Birmingham. He was a member of the Pilkington Committee on Broadcasting.

Holland, Henry Richard Fox, third Lord (1773-1840). Trained as a politician by his uncle, Charles James Fox. He opposed the Slave Trade, the severity of the criminal code and the Corn Laws. He and his wife made Holland House a centre for the wit and intellect of the age.

Howard, John (1726-1790). On a voyage of pleasure to Lisbon, he was captured by the French and imprisoned. This experience of the misery of the prisoner's life turned him into an earnest and untiring prison reformer. He died from typhus caught in visiting prisons in Russia.

Huddleston, Trevor (contemporary). Bishop of Masasi, Tanganyika (1960). Member of the Community of the Resurrection at Mirfield. Champion of the African Negro.

Huxley, Thomas Henry (1825-1895). Famous biologist. Supported Darwin in his theory of evolution.

James, William (1842-1910). Psychologist and philosopher, whose style of writing is particularly attractive, lucid and distinguished, and whose philosophy is wide and sensitive. Brother of Henry James.

Jaspers, Karl (contemporary). Professor of Philosophy at Heidelberg. Deprived of his chair in 1937. After the war lectured at Basle till 1961.

Jeffrey, Francis (1773-1850). One of the founders and editor of *Edinburgh Review*.

John XXIII (1881-1963). Pope 1958-63.

John of Salisbury (1117-1180). Friend of Thomas à Becket. Bishop of Chartres. "He had all the virtues of a humanist and none of his vices."

Kennedy, Alexander (1847-1928). Professor of Engineering, explored Petra and published the most complete monograph upon its history. Enthusiastic amateur musician.

Lamb, Mary (1764-1847). Sister of Charles Lamb. Suffered from recurring fits of insanity but when well was a singularly equable and sensible person with a lively wit and great intelligence. Author with Lamb, of *Tales from Shakespeare*, *Mrs. Leicester's School* and *Poems for Children*.

Langland, William (born about 1332). Author of *Piers the Plowman*, a long allegorical poem showing deep sympathy with the poor.

Lao Tze. Founder of Taoism and author of the mystical book *Tao tê Ching*, which was written before the end of the third century B.C.

Lascelles, Mary (contemporary). Tutor in English Literature at Somerville College, Oxford.

Law, William (1686-1761). A disciple and exponent of Jacob Boehme, the mystic. His *Serious Call to a Devout and Holy Life* greatly influenced both Dr. Johnson and the Wesleys.

Lessing, Gotthold Ephraim (1729-1781). Philosopher and poet. His dramatic poem, *Nathan der Weisse*, has been described as "one of the noblest pleas for toleration ever written".

Locke, John (1632-1704). Philosopher, secretary and friend to the first Lord Shaftesbury. Best remembered for his *Essay concerning Human Understanding.*

Luthuli, Albert J. (contemporary). Known to all those seeking justice in South Africa as "Chief". President of the now banned African National Congress. Taught for some years at Adams College until elected to the Chieftainship of the Grotville Area. From 1954-56 confined to his farm in Natal. Assaulted by white hooligans in 1958. Again confined to his farm for five years. After Sharpeville detained in prison and played a large part in rallying the accused at the Treason Trials. Again the Government confined him till 1963. In 1960 he was awarded the Nobel Peace Prize and in consequence was subjected to extreme abuse from the Government. Throughout the campaign against him he has never been anti-white. He has, in fact, influenced not only his own people but large numbers of whites. He has resolutely refused to give way to racial bitterness and has held firmly to the policy of non-violence.

MacDonald, George (1824-1905). Ordained as a Congregational Minister but spent most of his life writing novels of Scotch life, and allegorical fairy tales for children and adults full of mystical imagination.

Macmurray, John (contemporary). Professor of Moral Philosophy, Edinburgh, till 1958. Author of many books.

Malory, Thomas (died about 1471). Imprisoned as a Lancastrian. His *Morte D'Arthur*, printed by Caxton, was called by Walter Scott "the best prose romance the English language can boast of".

Malthe-Bruun, Kim (1923-1945). Born in Canada, lived at Copenhagen. Cabin boy and seaman. Captured and put to death by the Gestapo.

Mandeville, Bernard (1670-1733). A Dutch born doctor practising in London. Wrote *Satires.*

Marvell, Andrew (1621-1678). Poet, scholar and politician. Latin secretary to Milton. Member of Parliament under Richard Cromwell and Charles II. Fought against intolerable and arbitrary government. He revered Cromwell but accepted the Restoration, though his privately circulated *Satires against Monarchy* endangered his life.

Maurice, F. D. (1805-1872). Lost his chair of Theology at King's College, London, because of unorthodox views. He was a leader of the Christian Socialist Movement and a founder of Queen's College for Women and the Working Man's College.

Maximus of Tyre. Very little is known of this Platonic Philosopher. He lived at Tyre during the reigns of the Antonines and Commodus and wrote dissertations of which forty-one are extant. I have used the translation of Thomas Taylor (1804), altering a word here and there.

Mazzini, Joseph (1805-1872). Italian patriot, liberal and idealist. He was associated with Cavour and Garibaldi in the liberation of Italy.

Mill, John Stuart (1806-1873). At first a Utilitarian, but the influence of poetry and a period of great unhappiness deepened and widened his philosophy. He adored his wife, championed the cause of women and hated all forms of tyranny.

Montaigne (1533-1592). Scholar, essayist and courtier. His fearless questioning mind exerted great influence. These extracts are taken from Florio's famous translation of 1603, which Shakespeare almost certainly would have read.

Morrell, Lady Ottoline (1873-1937). Hostess and patron of the Arts.

Muir, Edwin (1887-1959). Born in Orkney. Journalist, author, translator, poet. Professor of Poetry at Harvard 1955-56.

Murray, Gilbert (1866-1957). Regius Professor of Greek at Oxford. Author of books on Greek literature and thought and translator in verse of Greek drama. One of the founders of the League of Nations Union and its Chairman from 1922–38. Helped to build up the United Nations Association after the last war.

Newman, John Henry (1801–1890). Cardinal (1879). His mother was a Calvinist. Great preacher. Author of a number of *Tracts for the Times*. Received into the Roman Catholic Church (1845). Best remembered perhaps for his moving *Apologie pro Vita sua*. His humility and tolerance were in striking contrast to his contemporaries and opponents, Mauning and Ward. His attitude is comparable to that of the present Pope John.

Niebuhr, Reinhold (contemporary). American theologian and sociologist. Professor of Christian Ethics and Philosophy of Religion at New York.

Osborne, Dorothy (1627–1695). Of a Royalist family. She fell in love with Sir William Temple, whose father was a Parliamentarian. They were faithful to one another, and Dorothy's delightful letters to Temple during a period of separation and difficulty before their marriage have luckily been preserved.

Pascal, Blaise (1623–1662). Saint and mathematician. Closely associated with the community of Port Royal though never a member. Defended the Jansenists against the Jesuits in his Provincial Letters, but is best remembered for his unfinished *Pensées*.

Pearsall Smith, Mrs. H. (1832–1911). She made a name for herself as a religious writer under the initials H. W. S. Born Hannah Whitall, of a strict Philadelphian Quaker family, she married a popular revivalist preacher, and became the mother of Logan Pearsall Smith, the author, and of two daughters, one of whom married Bertrand Russell (as his first wife) and the other Bernard Berenson.

Pelz, Werner (contemporary). Born in Berlin, now vicar of a church in Bolton.

Prewett, Frank (1893-1962). Farmer and poet. Described by Siegfried Sassoon in *Siegfried's Journey* as "a remarkable character with a streak of genius". In the second World War he was in command of operational research as Principal Scientific Officer for the R.A.F. in India and Singapore. The subject of this letter (aged 23 at his death) worked under Prewett in the R.A.F. for two years.

Priestley, Joseph (1733-1804). Unitarian minister, political philosopher, and scientist. Unfairly called atheist, he considered himself to hold the faith of the Primitive Christians. Wrote a history of electricity and discovered oxygen, and was elected to the French and Russian Academies of Science. He wrote a reply to Burke's *Reflections on the French Revolution* that led to a reactionary mob breaking into his house and destroying all his scientific instruments and books. He was driven from England to spend the rest of his life in America.

Reynolds, Reginald (1905-1958). Journalist and author. He came from a Somersetshire Quaker family and described himself as "a firebrand to the Quakers and a crank to the politicians . . . the most choleric pacifist in the British Isles". He made two visits to India and to Gandhi's Ashram, and was the chosen bearer to Lord Irwin of the letter which was the prelude to Civil Disobedience.

Rufinus (born between 340 and 345, died 410). Lived first in Egypt and then Palestine. He was a close friend of Jerome until they differed over a doctrinal controversy. Rufinus was considered dangerously unorthodox. Translator of Origen and author of *Historia Eremitica*, the lives of thirty-three Desert Fathers.

Rutherford, Mark [William Hale White], (1831-1913). Congregational Minister, expelled for unorthodoxy, he became a journalist and novelist.

Sayers, Dorothy (1893-1957). Dramatist, detective novelist, religious essayist and translator of Dante.

Schweitzer, Albert (contemporary). Musician, philosopher and missionary doctor in Equatorial Africa.

Seraphim of Sarov, St. (born about 1760, died 1833). Russian monk.

Sengai (1750-1837). Zen philosopher, Buddhist monk and artist.

Shaftesbury, Anthony Ashley Cooper, 7th Earl (1801-1885). Philanthropist. Promoted bills in Parliament for the better treatment of the insane, for the prevention of employment of "climbing boys", and for limiting hours of labour for women and children in factories. He supported the repeal of the Corn Laws and worked for the Ragged School Movement and better housing for the working class.

Smart, Christopher (1722-1771). Poet. Suffered from insanity. Befriended by Dr. Johnson. Some of his short lyrics are remarkably similar to Blake's, though there is no evidence that they knew of each other. His best known work is his *Song of David.*

Smith, Sydney (1771-1845). Anglican clergyman. One of the founders of the *Edinburgh Review.* Became a canon of St. Paul's. A witty, liberal-minded, kind and sensible man who did everyone good by making them laugh a great deal.

Sterne, Laurence (1713-1768). Clergyman and author of *Tristram Shandy* and *A Sentimental Journey.*

Street, Ethel (Mrs. Morris Ginsberg), (1898-1962). Poet and teacher.

Tawney, R. H. (1880-1962). Taught for many years in the W.E.A. Professor of Economic History, London. Fellow of Balliol. An inspired teacher and author of three influential books—*The Acquisitive Society, Religion and the Rise of Capitalism* and *Equality.*

Taylor, Jeremy (1613-1667). Author of Holy Living and "Holy Dying". Chaplain to Royalist Forces. Three times imprisoned. At Restoration he was made Bishop of an Irish See.

Temple, William (1881-1944). Archbishop of Canterbury.

Thucydides (471 to about 401 B.C.). Great Athenian historian of the Peloponnesian War.

Thurber, James (1894-1962). American journalist and author. On the staff of the *New Yorker.*

Tourville, Abbé de (1842-1903). Owing to ill health he spent most of his life in retirement, yet his influence among those who knew him was great. He was particularly interested in the study of social science.

Traherne, Thomas (1636?-1674). One of the most joyful of mystics. His poems and his wonderful prose work *Centuries of Meditation* were discovered by Bertram Dobell early in the present century.

Ullmann, Richard K. (contemporary). Ph.D.Frankfurt, German refugee from Nazism. Was interned at Buchenwald. A Quaker and now Associate Lecturer at Woodbrooke, and specially engaged in furthering the relationships of Christians in East and West Europe.

Underhill, Evelyn (Mrs. Stuart Moore), (1875-1941). Author of many religious books.

Upanishads, The. Part of the collection of Hindu sacred writings. This particular work deals with the nature of the Brahma or Supreme Spirit, "the being who is in his essence the light and life of all". The passage included here is from a translation by Tagore.

Vaughan, Henry (1622-1695). Poet and doctor. Influenced by George Herbert, but his best religious poems have an unsurpassed mystical beauty of their own.

Voltaire, François (1694-1778). Satirist and dramatist. Embroiled for most of his life with the Church and the Government of France. Attacked tyranny but also attacked Christianity. Admired greatly the English form of Government and the English Deists. Lived at Ferney near Geneva for the latter part of his long life.

Warren, Earl (contemporary). Chief Justice, U.S.A.

Whichcote, Benjamin (1609-1683). Cambridge Platonist. Provost of King's College, Cambridge.

Whitehead, Alfred North (1861-1947). Mathematician and philosopher at London and Harvard universities.

Williams, Charles (1886-1945). Poet, novelist and religious dramatist.

Wilson, Leonard (contemporary). Bishop of Singapore 1941-49. Interned Changi Camp, Singapore, 1943-45.

Winstanley, Gerard. Exact dates unknown, but in 1649 was a leader of "the Diggers", a branch of the Leveller movement, the first true socialist party in England. The Diggers were so called from their efforts to cultivate the waste places of England for the benefit of the poor. Winstanley appealed for the people's right to the Commons. He called himself a Universalist.

Woolman, John (1720-1772). A New England Quaker who was one of the first to recognize the evils of slavery. He also wrote and worked on behalf of the Red Indians and for all the exploited with whom he came in contact. He died, on a visit to England, from smallpox caught while investigating conditions among the poor weavers of York.

Wortley Montague, Lady Mary (1689-1762). Friend of Addison and Pope. Lived at Constantinople while her husband was ambassador there and wrote "Letters" from the East. Introduced inoculation for smallpox into England.

ACKNOWLEDGMENTS

ACKNOWLEDGMENTS

The following copyright material appears in this book, and I am grateful to all copyright-holders for permission to reprint the relevant passages. While I have taken every care to identify copyright-holders, I apologize if, by chance, any such should have been omitted.

ANSELM, ST. From Coulton's *Medieval Garner* (Cambridge University Press).

BARBELLION, W. P. N. From *Enjoying Life* (Chatto & Windus).

BEAUSOBRE, JULIA DE. From *The Woman Who Could Not Die* (Gollancz).

BEERBOHM, MAX. From *And Even Now* (Heinemann).

BRUM, MALTHE. From *Dying We Live* (Harvill Press).

BUDDHA, THE. Quoted in Tagore's *Sádhaná, The realisation of Life*, and presumably translated by him. I am grateful to the Trustees of the Tagore Estate as well as to Messrs. Macmillan for permission.

BUTTERFIELD, HERBERT. From a Robert Waley Cohen Lecture (The Council of Christians and Jews).

CHARDIN, PIERRE DE. From *Letters of a Traveller* and *Le Milieu Divin* (Collins).

CHING, TAO TÊ. From *Analects of Confucius* tr. by Arthur Waley (Allen & Unwin).

CURTIS, LIONEL. From *Civitas Dei* (Allen & Unwin).

DOLCI, DANILO. From *Waste* (MacGibbon & Kee).

DOSTOEVSKY. From *The Brothers Karamazov* tr. by Constance Garnett (Heinemann).

ERASMUS. Certain passages are from Huizinga's *Erasmus of Rotterdam* (Phaidon Press).

FORSTER, E. M. From *A Passage to India* (Edward Arnold).

FRY, CHRISTOPHER. From *The Dark Is Light Enough* (Oxford University Press).

GANDHI, MAHATMA. From *Gandhi: An Autobiography* (The Navajivan Trust, Ahmedabad).

GRIMBLE, SIR ARTHUR. From *A Pattern of Islands* (John Murray).

HASELDEN, KYLE. From *The Racial Problem in Christian Perspective* (Lutterworth Press).

HEATH, RACHEL. I thank Miss Rachel Heath for permission to quote from an unpublished address.

HILL, A. V. From *The Ethical Dilemma of Science* (Oxford University Press, New York).

HIS HOLINESS POPE JOHN XXIII. From *Peace on Earth*, an Encyclical Letter of Pope John XXIII (Catholic Truth Society, London).

HOGGART, RICHARD. From *The Uses of Literacy* (Chatto & Windus).

HUDDLESTONE, TREVOR. From *Naught for Your Comfort* (Collins).

JASPERS, KARL. From *The Origin and Goal of History* (Routledge & Kegan Paul).

JUNG, C. G. From *Modern Man In Search of a Soul* tr. by W. S. Dell and Cary F. Baynes (Routledge & Kegan Paul).

LASCELLES, MARY. From *Jane Austen* (Clarendon Press).

LIVINGSTONE, SIR RICHARD. From a Robert Waley Cohen Lecture (The Council of Christians and Jews).

MACMURRAY, JOHN. From *The Clue to History* (S.C.M. Press).

MUIR, EDWIN. From *Collected Poems* (Faber & Faber).

MURRAY, GILBERT. From *The Rise of the Greek Epic* and *Five Stages of Greek Religion* (Clarendon Press).

OTTOLINE. From *Ottoline: The Early Memoirs (1873-1915) of Lady Ottoline Morrell* ed. by R. Gathorne-Hardy (Faber & Faber).

PELZ, WERNER. From *God Is No More* (Gollancz).

PLATO. I thank the Trustees of the Jowett Copyright Fund for permission to use Jowett's translation.

REYNOLDS, REGINALD. From *The Wisdom of John Woolman* (Allen & Unwin).

SAYERS, DOROTHY L. From *The Zeal of Thy House* (Gollancz).

SCHWEITZER, ALBERT. From *Civilization and Ethics* (A. & C. Black).

SERAPHIM OF SAROV, ST. From *St. Seraphim of Sarov* tr. by A. F. Dobbie-Bateman (S.P.C.K.).

SHAW, G. B. From the Preface to *On The Rocks*, from *Misalliance*, from *St. Joan*, from the Preface to *Getting Married*, and from the Preface to *Imprisonment*. I thank the Public Trustee and The Society of Authors.

SMITH, LOGAN PEARSALL. From *A Religious Rebel* (James Nisbet).

STAFFORD-CLARK, DR. DAVID. From a Robert Waley Cohen Lecture (The Council of Christians and Jews).

TAWNEY, R. H. From *Religion and the Rise of Capitalism* (John Murray).

TEMPLE, WILLIAM. From *Repton School Sermons*. I am grateful to Messrs. Macmillan and to Mrs. William Temple for permission.

TERESA, ST. From *The Way of Perfection* and from *The Interior Castle*. Both tr. by E. A. Peers (Sheed & Ward).

THOMAS, F. W. From *History of India* (Cambridge University Press).

THURBER, JAMES. From *Lanterns and Lances* (Hamish Hamilton). I am grateful to Messrs. Harper & Row of New York for Canadian permission. I also thank Mrs. James Thurber.

TOLSTOY. From *Where Love Is God Is* tr. by A. Maude (Oxford University Press), and from *Resurrection* tr. by Louise Maude (Oxford University Press).

TOURVILLE, ABBÉ DE. From *Letters of Direction* tr. by Lucy Menzies (Dacre Press: A. & C. Black, Ltd.).

TRAHERNE. From *Poems* (Clarendon Press).

ULLMANN, RICHARD. From his *Swarthmore Lecture* (Society of Friends). My thanks are due to the late Richard Ullmann.

UNDERHILL, EVELYN. From *Concerning the Inner Life: The House of the Soul* (Methuen).

WADDELL, HELEN. From her translation of *The Desert Fathers* (Constable).

WEBB, BEATRICE. From *My Apprenticeship* (Longmans, Green).

WEDGWOOD, C. V. From *William the Silent* (Cape).

WEST, MORRIS. From *Children of the Sun* (Heinemann).

WHITEHEAD, A. N. From *Science and the Modern World* (Cambridge University Press).

WILLIAMS, CHARLES. From *The Image of the City* (Oxford University Press), from *The Descent of the Dove* (Faber & Faber), and from *The English Poetic Mind* (Clarendon Press).

WILSON, THE RIGHT REV. JOHN L., BISHOP OF BIRMINGHAM. From a broadcast given on 13th October, 1946.

For the extract from Charles Booth's Memoir by his wife, I thank Messrs. Macmillan.

I thank Fr. Jennifer Thomassen for a translation from the old Dutch of Dirk Volckertzoon Coornhert.

INDEX

INDEX